The Key To AUTISM

An Evidence-based Workbook for Assessing and Treating Children & Adolescents

Practical Strategies for Organization, Social Communication,
Self-regulation, and Solving Challenging Behaviors

Cara Marker Daily, PhD

"Dr. Daily's book is written with remarkable clarity, and will be a wonderful, frequently used resource for professionals, parents, and learners with autism. She provides a unique blend of conceptual and practical information, with an up-to-date account of the DSM-5 and all details related to coding. Her perspective of the way people with autism process information is a testament to her extensive professional experience and her understanding of living, thinking and breathing with autism. Dr. Daily's case studies, valuable teaching tips, and elaborate resources are a true gift to this field."

- Aletta Sinoff, PhD, CCC-SLP, BCBA-D, COBA

"Dr. Daily has put together an excellent collection of best practices for working with children with autism. Therapists, educators and parents will value the detailed interventions as well as the excellent case studies and worksheets."

- Teresa Garland, MOT, OTR/L
Author of *Self-Regulation Interventions and Strategies*

"*Key to Autism* is a must-read for professionals working in the field of autism and Dr. Daily has much to share in her 20+ years of experience working alongside individuals with ASD. It is three books in one – a handbook about autism, an overview of empirically supported treatments, and an applied treatment workbook – she has left no stone unturned!"

- Tracy Masterson, PhD
Licensed Clinical Psychologist

"While Dr. Cara Daily wrote *The Key to Autism* as a guide for professionals who assess and treat children and teens with autism spectrum disorders, her extraordinarily clear and practical style of communication has resulted in a book for anyone...parents, educators or family members seeking to fully understand the "whys" and "hows" of a much misunderstood condition. *The Key to Autism* offers as clear and concise a summary of evidence-based practices for evaluation and treatment as one could hope for."

- Stephen Grcevich, MD
Division of Child and Adolescent Psychiatry
Case Western Reserve University School of Medicine
President and Founder, Key Ministry

"Having been an educator for more than forty years, I am so glad to have Dr. Cara Daily as a colleague. Her ability to reach autistic children is amazing. This book is a fabulous resource for professionals in the autism community. It is well written and easy to understand with both an explanation of ASD and treatments that really work."

- Carole Richards
President, North Coast Education Service

Copyright © 2016 by Cara Marker Daily

Published by
PESI Publishing & Media
PESI, Inc
3839 White Ave
Eau Claire, WI 54703

Cover: Amy Rubenzer
Editing: Kara Ruesch
Layout: Bookmasters & Amy Rubenzer

ISBN: 9781559570534

Printed in the United States of America.

PESI
Publishing
& Media
www.pesipublishing.com

Contents

About the Author

Cara Marker Daily, PhD, is a licensed pediatric psychologist with over 20 years of experience with autism in home, school, hospital, and community settings. She works directly with educators, speech/language pathologists, occupational therapists, BCBAs, and other professionals. Dr. Daily is president and training director of Daily Behavioral Health, a leading behavioral health provider in northeast Ohio specializing in assessment, consultation, and treatment of autism, anxiety, and disruptive behavior disorders. Dr. Daily is also founder and executive director of the Building Behaviors Autism Center, which has received numerous grants to provide free and reduced-cost applied behavioral analysis services to individuals with autism. She has written several cognitive-behavioral and behavioral-based curriculums focusing on teaching daily living skills to children with autism and published a peer-reviewed journal article supporting evidence for success of these programs. She has presented nationally on autism, disruptive behaviors disorder, anxiety, and chronic health conditions in the pediatric population. Dr. Daily has been featured in radio, television, and other media platforms in northeast Ohio.

Dr. Daily received her Ph.D. in School Psychology at the University of South Carolina, and completed an internship in Pediatric Psychology at the Children's Hospital of Philadelphia and a postdoctoral fellowship in Pediatric Psychology at The Children's Hospital at The Cleveland Clinic. Dr. Daily is a member of the Department of Pediatrics at Fairview Hospital at the Cleveland Clinic, the American Psychological Association, the Ohio Psychological Association, the Society of Pediatric Psychology, and the Christian Association of Psychological Studies.

Acknowledgements

LEARNING TO LOVE AUTISM

I did not always love working with autism. I cried a lot in the beginning. I first began working with autism while I was an undergraduate at Kalamazoo College in Michigan. I majored in psychology and secondary education. My first exposure to autism was obtained through the college's career development program, when I became a paraprofessional at a local school for children with moderate to severe physical and intellectual disabilities.

As a paraprofessional, I was exposed to many different students, teachers, professionals, and programs. Depending upon the hour, part of my job was to move children with severe traumatic brain injury from their wheelchairs to tilt tables and to change their diapers. At other times, I worked with low functioning students with autism on completing certain self-help skill tasks. I didn't know it at the time, but I was actually using techniques of applied behavioral analysis (ABA) with the students. The first two weeks working at this school were exhausting. I cried every night and remember telling my parents on the phone that this was something I did not want to do in the future. That's when I decided to go to graduate school instead.

After interviewing at several different universities, I decided to go to the University of South Carolina for my Ph.D. in School Psychology. At first, I began studying the Quality of Life of individuals with intellectual disabilities, but my heart was just not into the research. I did not love it. I then decided to turn my interests to the more chronic health populations. I began working with low birth weight infants, sickle cell disease, HIV, and oncology. I absolutely loved it. Having a close friend die of leukemia in high school was one of the reasons I think I was drawn to the more chronic health population.

Interestingly enough, I still didn't get away from children with neurodevelopmental disorders. During my last two years of graduate school, I worked at a residential treatment facility for children with autism and other special needs. I conducted comprehensive assessments for autism and evaluated teachers, speech language pathologists, and other staff on following ABA programs that we created for the students. I enjoyed my time at the residential school, but still did not love autism.

After completing my coursework and practicum experiences in graduate school, I completed a predoctoral internship at Children's Hospital of Philadelphia, working mostly with children awaiting heart/lung and/or kidney transplant and children with cancer. It was during this time I worked a lot with palliative care and experienced some amazing relationships with families and staff as they lost loves ones due to cancer or heart/lung failure.

The following year, I continued my studies, accepting a postdoctoral fellowship at the Children's Hospital at the Cleveland Clinic in Ohio. Most of my work was in oncology and cardiology again, but I also began to do a little with autism as the Cleveland Clinic had a state-of-the-art Center for Autism program, focused on discrete trial training (DTT) with children with autism.

Throughout these years, I still felt like I did not know what I was supposed to do in this life. As I worked, I also began traveling throughout the world. I went on several short-term mission trips to Ireland, Mexico, Africa, and Brazil, as well as smaller trips in the United States. After I finished my postdoctoral fellowship at the Cleveland

Clinic, I literally received a phone call from a friend of a friend, who said he had a small medical building across from one of the Cleveland Clinic hospitals. He told me that he had heard I may need office space. I didn't even know what I needed space for and I couldn't afford anything, but he was insistent that I come check it out. He said he and his wife prayed about the space and felt they were supposed to let me do whatever it is I was supposed to do in that space until I was able to pay. Crazy, right? When I checked out the space, it had three small treatment rooms, a kitchen, a receptionist area, and a waiting room. I told the owner of the building that it was too much space, and he told me that maybe I was to fill the space. So, I did. I started my own business and literally one month later, a wonderful woman finishing up her doctorate in psychology walked through my door asking me if I would want to supervise her, then another month later, another wonderful woman, a psychologist, came in, and this just kept happening until we were so big that we had to take additional office space from the owner of the building until we finally had to buy our own building. All this happened in less than 7 years. We started trying to work with the more chronically ill populations, but we kept getting referrals to evaluate and work with children with autism and other neurodevelopmental disorders. There apparently were not many people trained in working with this population 15+ years ago.

When I got married, I took my husband's last name of "Daily" and changed the name of our business to Daily Behavioral Health. I liked the dual use of the name. Now, we operate out of an old Catholic Convent on the West side of Cleveland. We have approximately 15+ service providers in the fields of psychology, speech/language pathology, counseling, and behavior therapy. We also have several other locations across Northeast Ohio. We provide services to children as young as 12 months of age through adulthood. Our specialties are in comprehensive evaluations, individual and family treatment, home and school consultations, and group therapy.

We also started a nonprofit organization, the Building Behaviors Autism Center several years ago as a way to provide free and reduced cost services to those families with autism. Typically it costs a child with autism $20,000 to $70,000 a year to receive any type of services focused on ABA. Since it was difficult to find any type of affordable research-based intervention in Northeast Ohio, the Building Behaviors Autism Center began. It was started as a result of a substantial anonymous grant from someone in the community and has continued as a result of grants from Community West Foundation, In His Steps Foundation, and others. The Building Behaviors Autism Center continues to grow and shows God's love in a radical way by providing free and affordable services to families of individuals with autism.

Throughout the years of working with this population, my love for autism grew. My brain is very analytical and I love puzzles. Every individual, whether they are neurotypical or have autism, is very different. I love coming to work each day as I experience something different every second I am there. Individuals with autism tend to live in the present and they have taught me to do the same. I like to say to others that I was first friends with autism before I fell in love with autism, but it's a love that will last a lifetime.

Thank you to all the families and children with whom I have worked with for 20+ years. You have taught me more than I could ever have imagined and have blessed my life. A special acknowledgement goes to those professionals at Daily Behavioral Health and the Building Behaviors Autism Center for working with me in creating programs that make a difference in our community. Thank you to all the educational institutions and mentors who have given me the foundation to grow in this love for autism. A special thank you to my family for joining me on this roller coaster ride that has become our life, which we genuinely love. Lastly, I thank the Lord for giving me the strength and courage to walk through the doors that He opened for me to work with these amazing families.

How to Use This Book

The goal is to give every professional the necessary tools to work with an individual with autism. This workbook will give you the latest research, but more importantly provides you with an easy-to-read guide with many case examples and hands-on exercises to better understand the brain of an individual with autism. It also includes tools for screening and assessment as well as "how-to" sections for applied behavioral analysis (ABA), social communication, decreasing repetitive behaviors, creating a positive environment, and teaching self-regulation strategies.

As a comprehensive manual, there are two parts to this book. **Part One** is focused on the research. Understanding the history, conceptualization, and research will help professionals discover what it is like to have a brain with autism. **Part Two** is focused on the strategies. It includes easy-to-use practical techniques, as well as skill-building exercises, worksheets, and resources. Many of these strategies are useful for therapists in both group or individual therapy settings.

This book will help professionals integrate research with practical strategies that will set up individuals with autism for success. Professionals will add to their tool box numerous techniques that are easy to implement and which promote positive relationships with individuals with autism.

Part One

Chapter ONE

Autism and Other Neurodevelopmental Disorders

THE HISTORY OF AUTISM AND THE DSM

One question I am always asked as soon as I say I work with children with autism is, "Has autism always been around?" The answer to that question is yes; we just used to call it something different. In 1952, the Diagnostic Statistical Manual of Mental Disorders (DSM) was created by the American Psychiatric Association Committee on Nomenclature and Statistics to collect statistical information about mental disorders and was later used to assist psychiatrists, psychologists, and other mental health professionals in diagnosing specific mental disorders. When the DSM was first published, autism was just called, "Schizophrenic reaction - childhood type."

1952	1968	1980	1987	1994	2000	2013
DSM-I	DSM-II	DSM-III	DSM-III-R	DSM-IV	DSM-IV-TR	DSM-5

DSM-I: Schizophrenic Reaction (Childhood Type)

DSM-II: Schizophrenic Reaction (Childhood Type)

DSM-III: Pervasive Developmental Disorders:
• Childhood Onset PDD
• Infantile Autism
• Atypical Autism

DSM-III-R: Pervasive Developmental Disorders:
• PDD-NOS
• Autistic Disorder

DSM-IV: Pervasive Developmental Disorders:
• PDD-NOS
• Autistic Disorder
• Asperger Disorder
• Rett Syndrome
• Childhood Disintegrative Disorder

DSM-IV-TR: Pervasive Developmental Disorders:
• PDD-NOS
• Autistic Disorder
• Asperger Disorder
• Rett Syndrome
• Childhood Disintegrative Disorder

DSM-5: Neurodevelopmental Disorders:
• Intellectual Disability
• Communication Disorders
• Autism Spectrum Disorder
• Attention-Deficit/Hyperactivity Disorder
• Specific Learning Disorder
• Motor Disorders

Daily, C. (2014)

In 1980, the DSM-III created a new category of Pervasive Developmental Disorders (PDD). Let's analyze the phrase pervasive developmental disorder. "Pervasive," which means throughout. "Developmental" is defined as occurring before the age of three and continuing on throughout adulthood. "Disorder," which in this case, means an impairment. A disorder does not mean a delay. This is a hard concept for many of our families to accept and understand. Children with developmental delays may catch up in certain aspects, whereas children with pervasive developmental disorders do not. A disorder means there is an impairment or a disruption. Something is different.

■ *Conversation with a Pioneer in the Field of Autism* ■

It's amazing all the wonderful people I have met as I have traveled throughout the US presenting on autism. At one presentation in Philadelphia, I met a wonderful older gentleman who attended an all-day conference of mine. At one of the breaks, he came up to me and asked me if I knew the name Leo Kanner. I said, "Well, yes, but I never got the chance to meet him." Leo Kanner was one of the first psychiatrists to specialize in children with autism. In 1943, he published "Autistic Disturbances of Affective Contact" which became a foundational paper in our understanding of autism today. This older man at the conference then began to tell me that he worked with Kanner and his predecessors at John Hopkins Hospital in the 1950s. I wish I could have recorded this wonderful pioneer in the field of autism as he told me numerous stories of how they would treat autism in their clinic. He described how they would rock and bottle feed adults wearing diapers in rocking chairs. He commented that they really did not know how to treat them, but based on the "refrigerator mother" hypothesis, a hypothesis later rejected, they attempted to use treatment techniques that would model an attachment relationship in the early developmental period (Kanner, 1943). This man was astonished how far the field in ASD has grown in the last 70 years. It was a pleasure meeting this gentleman and I commend him and others who worked with this population long ago.

During this time, they also began using the term "autism." Specifically, there was childhood onset PDD, infantile autism, and atypical autism. It was not until 1994, when the DSM-IV was created, that under the category of PDD, they classified autism, Asperger's disorder, PDD-NOS, Rett's syndrome, and childhood disintegrative disorder. Asperger's disorder was named after Hans Asperger, who published a paper in 1944 describing four boys who had difficulties with empathy, coordination, and forming friendships. When engaged in conversations, they were typically one-sided and many times would talk like "little professors" given their intense interest in certain subjects. Rett's syndrome and childhood disintegrative disorder were classified as pervasive developmental disorders, as both of these disorders are characterized as having normal early development followed by a severe loss of skills, which in some cases may present itself as looking like an autism spectrum disorder.

In 2013, the DSM-5 was published. There were some major changes that occurred with this revision. First, instead of the Roman numeral V, they used the number 5. As funny as this may sound, this is a big deal. Basically, the thought is that they will be revising the DSM-5 and it is easy to revise numerically using the number 5 (e.g., 5.1, 5.2, 5.3, etc.).

Second, instead of the category of pervasive developmental disorders, they added a broader category called "Neurodevelopmental Disorders." Think about the phrase "neurodevelopmental disorder." "Neuro," meaning something is occurring in the brain. "Developmental," meaning something that occurs early on and continues throughout adulthood. "Disorder" meaning it is not a delay, but some sort of impairment. Within this category of neurodevelopmental disorders, the DSM-5 groups together all disorders that contain some sort of brain impairment that occurs early on in the developmental period. The six disorders include: intellectual disabilities, communication disorders, autism spectrum disorders, ADHD, specific learning disorders, and motor disorders.

AUTISM AND THE DSM-IV

The next question I usually hear is, "How did the symptoms of autism disorder change from the DSM-IV to the DSM-5?" To better understand how all the symptoms from the DSM-IV load into the new DSM-5, a visual aide has been provided. In the DSM-IV, there are three categories of symptoms, which include impairments in social interaction, communication, and restrictive repetitive and stereotyped patterns of behaviors.

DSM IV: Autistic Disorder

299.00 (F84.0)
Diagnostic Criteria

DSM 5: Autistic Spectrum Disorder

A. Total of six (or more) items from (1), (2), and (3), with at least two from (1), and one each from (2) and (3):

3. Qualitative impairment in social interaction, as manifested by at least two of the following:

(a) Marked impairment in the use of multiple nonverbal behaviors such as eye-to-eye gaze, facial expression, body postures, and gestures to regulate social interaction

(b) Failure to develop peer relationships appropriate to developmental level

(c) A lack of spontaneous seeking to share enjoyment, interests, or achievements with other people

(d) Lack of social or emotional reciprocity

2. Qualitative impairments in communication as manifested by at least one of the following:

(a) Delay in, or total lack of, the development of spoken language (not accompanied by an attempt to compensate through alternative modes of communication such as gesture or mime)

(b) In individuals with adequate speech, marked impairment in the ability to initiate or sustain a conversation with others

(c) Stereotyped and repetitive use of language or idiosyncratic language

(d) Lack of varied, spontaneous make-believe play or social imitative play appropriate to developmental level

1. Restricted repetitive and stereotyped patterns of behavior, interests, and activities, as manifested by at least one of the following:

(a) Encompassing preoccupation with one or more stereotyped and restricted patterns of interest that is abnormal either in intensity or focus

(b) Apparently inflexible adherence to specific, nonfunctional routines or rituals

(c) Stereotyped and repetitive motor mannerisms (e.g., hand or finger flapping or twisting, or complex whole-body movements)

(d) Persistent preoccupation with parts of objects

Specify current severity: Severity is based on social communication impairments and restricted repetitive patterns of behavior (see Table 2).

A. Persistent deficits in social communication and social interaction across multiple contexts, as manifested by the following, currently or by history (examples are illustrative, not exhaustive; see text):

1. Deficits in social-emotional reciprocity, ranging, for example, from abnormal social approach and failure of normal back-and-forth conversation; to reduced sharing of interests, emotions, or affect; to failure to initiate or respond to social interactions.

2. Deficits in nonverbal communicative behaviors used for social interaction, ranging, for example, from poorly integrated verbal and nonverbal communication; to abnormalities in eye contact and body language or deficits in understanding and use of gestures; to a total lack of facial expressions and nonverbal communication.

3. Deficits in developing, maintaining, and understanding relationships, ranging, for example, from difficulties adjusting behavior to suit various social contexts; to difficulties in sharing imaginative play or in making friends; to absence of interest in peers.

Specify current severity: Severity is based on social communication impairments and restricted repetitive patterns of behavior (see Table 2).

B. Restricted, repetitive patterns of behavior, interests, or activities, as manifested by at least two of the following, currently or by history (examples are illustrative, not exhaustive; see text):

1. Stereotyped or repetitive motor movements, use of objects, or speech (e.g., simple motor stereotypes, lining up toys or flipping objects, echolalia, idiosyncratic phrases).

2. Insistence on sameness, inflexible adherence to routines, or ritualized patterns of verbal or nonverbal behavior (e.g., extreme distress at small changes, difficulties with transitions, rigid thinking patterns, greeting rituals, need to take same route or eat same food every day).

3. Highly restricted, fixated interests that are abnormal in intensity or focus (e.g., strong attachment to or preoccupation with unusual objects, excessively circumscribed or perseverative interests).

4. Hyper- or hyporeactivity to sensory input or unusual interest in sensory aspects of the environment (e.g. apparent indifference to pain/temperature, adverse response to specific sounds or textures, excessive smelling or touching of objects, visual fascination with lights or movement).

C. Delays or abnormal functioning in at least one of the following areas, with onset prior to age 3 years: (1) social interaction, (2) language as used in social communication, or (3) symbolic or imaginative play.

D. The disturbance is not better accounted for by Rett's Disorder or Childhood Disintegrative Disorder

C. Symptoms must be present in the early developmental period (but may not become fully manifest until social demands exceed limited capacities, or may be masked by learned strategies in later life).

D. Symptoms cause clinically significant impairment in social, occupational, or other important areas of current functioning.

E. These disturbances are not better explained by intellectual disability (intellectual developmental disorder) or global developmental delay. Intellectual disability and autism spectrum disorder frequently co-occur; to make comorbid diagnoses of autism spectrum disorder and intellectual disability, social communication should be below that expected for general developmental level.

Note: Individuals with a well-established DSM-IV diagnosis of autistic disorder, Asperger's disorder, or pervasive developmental disorder not otherwise specified should be given the diagnosis of autism spectrum disorder. Individuals who have marked deficits in social communication, but whose symptoms do not otherwise meet criteria for autism spectrum disorder, should be evaluated for social (pragmatic) communication disorder.

Becomes a specifier

Specify if:

With or without accompanying intellectual impairment. With or without accompanying language impairment. Associated with a known medical or genetic condition or environmental factor (Coding note: Use additional code to identify the associated medical or genetic condition.) Associated with another neurodevelopmental, mental, or behavioral disorder (Coding note: Use additional code(s) to identify the associated neurodevelopmental, mental, or behavioral disorder(s).) With catatonia (refer to the criteria for catatonia associated with another mental disorder, pp. 119-120, for definition) (Coding note: Use additional code 293.89 (F06.1) catatonia associated with autism spectrum disorder to indicate the presence of the comorbid catatonia.)

Social interaction

In the DSM-IV, individuals needed to show at least two qualitative impairments in the category of social interaction. First, an individual may show impairment in the use of nonverbal communication, such as eye contact or eye-to-eye gaze. Many times an individual with ASD may look above the eyes of another individual or they may not follow the other person's eyes when turning their head to look at a referenced object. They also may have a difficult time understanding facial expressions as well as gestures and body postures. As we will learn from the newer research in the next chapter, this is because there are numerous parts in the human face, which is difficult for any individual with ASD to understand. In addition, individuals with ASD may also have difficulty expressing themselves nonverbally. They may engage in more of a flat affect, where they may say they are happy, but their face may appear expressionless. They may have a hard time connecting what they are saying with their gestures. A lot of individuals with ASD may have difficulty telling or showing someone how to do a task at the same time.

Second, an individual with ASD may have difficulty developing friendships appropriate to developmental level. I always ask my children with ASD if they have friends and typically they will say yes. Then I ask their friends' names. They will either say, "I don't know" or they will begin naming off every child in their classroom. Their definition of a friend may just be someone they see on a daily basis. If they do have friends, many times their friendships are with others who are not their age.

> ### Case Example
> # GREG
>
> Greg is a three-year-old boy who spoke mostly one or two word utterances. He wondered around my room, squealing and smiling, although never made eye contact with his mother or me. He tightly gripped a green rubber Gumby character in his hands. When I asked if he could show me Gumby, Greg quickly swayed back and forth as he stood in front of me and repeated, "Show Gumby, show Gumby, show Gumby," but he did not show me Gumby. After our first session, I recommended a full comprehensive evaluation to assess for autism. A couple weeks later, Greg's mother came into my office with crutches. When I asked her what happened, she told me that she fell down the stairs and broke her leg. She continued by saying, "I'm not sure what hurt more, the actually pain of breaking my leg or the fact that Greg was at the bottom of the stairs and had no idea that I had fallen, broken my leg, and was in pain."

Other individuals with ASD may have difficulty sharing enjoyment or interests with others. If a typical two-year-old boy sees a plane in the sky, he will look at mom and say, "Look mom, a plane!" During this interaction, they usually make eye contact with their mother, establish joint attention, and point to the plane in the sky. The child is excited about seeing the plane and wants to share that excitement with his mother. A child with ASD may see the plane, but have no interest in sharing that excitement with another person or may be too engaged to even notice the plane.

The last symptom in the social interaction category is "lack of social or emotional reciprocity." This comes from the "theory of mind" concept, in which an individual with ASD may not be able to understand that others have beliefs or interests that are different than their own. I have heard some professionals call this "lack of empathy," although I have worked with many individuals with ASD who possess empathy. A better description is the individual with ASD has a hard time taking on another person's perspective.

Communication

Within impairments in communication, the DSM-IV required at least one impairment in four symptom categories. First, a "delay in, or total lack of, the development of spoken language" Some individuals with ASD, may be nonverbal, speak in only one or two word utterances, or only be able to use simple speech.

Secondly, some individuals with ASD, who do possess speech, may have difficulty initiating or sustaining a conversation with others. They may be impaired in the ability to greet others, engage in turn taking in play or conversations, or display a lack of reciprocal back and forth communication.

Individuals with ASD may also engage in stereotyped and repetitive language or idiosyncratic language. Echolalia may occur, which is when individuals repeat themselves or others. When individuals with ASD speak, you may notice some peculiar intonation in certain words or inappropriate voice tone and volume. They may also engage in pronoun reversals or use words out of context.

Lastly, some individuals with ASD may display impairments in "make-believe play or social imitative play appropriate to developmental level." A typical child, if given a toy car might pretend to drive the car and say "vroom, vroom." That same child should also be able to imitate others as well as engage in some back-and-forth play with another toy, such as a dinosaur stepping on and destroying the car. In comparison, a child with ASD may do nothing with the car or pick up the car and possibly spin the wheels or use it in some other nonfunctional way.

Case Example
JACKSON

Jackson is a five-year-old boy who presented for an evaluation. He was extremely verbal and talked excessively about space in great detail, although he did not engage in appropriate eye contact and only talked about his interests. While obtaining information about his developmental history, I asked his mother to describe his imaginative play skills. She described that when Jackson was two, he created Star Wars episodes 8, 9, and 10. Recently, he recorded all those episodes in several notebooks. At school, he sits in the back of the classroom and acts out each of these stories with hand movements and various noises. Jackson obviously has a great imagination and some turn-taking that occurs in his own play, although the play is not appropriate to his developmental level as it is focused on his own interests. He also has difficulty in turn taking in play and conversation with others. The comprehensive evaluation revealed that this child did meet criteria for an autism spectrum disorder, but he was also quite gifted, with an IQ of 152. As the years passed, Jackson became fluent and self-taught in both Japanese and Latin before the age of 12.

Repetitive and stereotyped behaviors

The last category in the DSM-IV for autism is what is called "restricted repetitive and stereotyped patterns of behavior, interests, and activities". A child with ASD must have one of four symptoms. The first symptom is some type of highly-fixated interest, such as a two-year-old child with ASD who can draw Marvel Comic Strips better than Stan Lee or the child who wrote the next Star Wars episodes before George Lucas. There is typically some interest that they perseverate on and may know information about the subject in great detail.

Their thinking may also be inflexible or rigid. They could have difficulties with changes in their routines and/or schedules. In conversations, they may have an impairment in the ability to understand more abstract language, such as metaphors, idioms, and sarcasm.

Some individuals with ASD may engage in "stereotyped and repetitive motor mannerisms" such as toe walking, hand flapping, head banging, arm biting, etc. Higher functioning individuals with ASD may exhibit some peculiar fine motor mannerisms, such as strange finger posturing.

Lastly, some individuals may display a preoccupation with certain parts of an object. For example, instead of drinking from a water glass served at a restaurant, an individual with ASD may "stim" off the stem of the glass. At our behavioral practice, we have round air conditioning vents that do not look like traditional air conditioning vents, so many times children with ASD go over to the vents and move their finger circularly around the vent. Many times, children with ASD become preoccupied with objects that they either may not understand, are fearful of, or enjoy a lot.

Case Example

JACOB

Jacob is a 10-year-old boy who was seen for a comprehensive evaluation to assess for Asperger's disorder. He initially walked in my office and said rather formerly, "Hello Dr. Daily. This is my mother and father. It is very nice to meet you." As I talked with him, Jacob asked me about what we do in therapy together. In response, I said, "Great question, you and I will put our heads together about that," to which he replied, "Ouch! That would hurt!" Although Jacob was able to greet others, he displayed several symptoms of inflexibility. He also had extreme difficulty maintaining friendships as he was very controlling and demanded that all the rules of games needed to be followed exactly. He was subsequently diagnosed with Asperger's disorder. After the evaluation, I had not seen him for approximately six months. When I saw him in the waiting room, I said, "Hey stranger!" Jacob then began to cry and said, "You don't remember me, you don't know my name!" I felt extremely bad and apologized. Then I explained that I did remember him and was just using sarcasm to say hello.

AUTISM AND THE DSM-5

In 2013, the DSM-5 diagnostic criteria for autism changed significantly. As you see in the DSM-IV and DSM-5 visual on page 5, all the symptoms from the DSM-IV load into the DSM-5, although instead of three symptom categories, there are now two: impairments in social communication and restricted, repetitive patterns of behavior. Communication impairments have been removed. This is because communication impairments are considered a different neurodevelopmental disorder. Many times, individuals were confusing general communication impairments with that of social communication impairments in autism. For example, an expressive or receptive language delay or articulation difficulties are not symptoms of autism. The symptoms of autism that relate to communication are only those focused on social interactions.

Social communication

In social communication, an individual with ASD needs to have all of the three symptoms in this category. This category is a combination of most of the symptoms (except stereotype and repetitive language) of Social Interaction and Communication in the DSM-IV. Individuals need to have deficits in social emotional reciprocity, deficits in nonverbal communication behaviors used for social interaction, and deficits in developing, maintaining and understanding relationships.

Restricted repetitive patterns of behavior

In the restricted repetitive patterns of behavior category, an individual with ASD needs to demonstrate two of the four categories of symptoms. They may display difficulties in stereotyped repetitive motor mannerisms and movements, insistence on sameness or being inflexible with routines, may have highly-restricted, fixated interest, that are abnormal in intensity, or may have a "hyper- or hyporeactivity to sensory input or unusual interest in sensory aspects of the environment." This last symptom of "hyper- or hyporeactivity to sensory input or unusual interest in sensory aspects of the environment" is a new addition to the DSM-5. According to the DSM-5, this may include "apparent indifference to pain/temperature, adverse response to specific sounds or textures, excessive smelling or touching of objects, visual fascination with lights or movement." We have always known that individuals with ASD experience different sensory input compared to typical individuals. Now the DSM-5 recognizes that.

DSM-5 ■ Autism Spectrum Disorder 299.00 (F84.0)

Diagnostic Criteria

A. Persistent deficits in social communication and social interaction across multiple contexts, as manifested by the following, currently or by history (examples are illustrative, not exhaustive, see text):

  1. Deficits in social-emotional reciprocity, ranging, for example, from abnormal social approach and failure of normal back-and-forth conversation; to reduced sharing of interests, emotions, or affect; to failure to initiate or respond to social interactions.

  2. Deficits in nonverbal communicative behaviors used for social interaction, ranging, for example, from poorly integrated verbal and nonverbal communication; to abnormalities in eye contact and body language or deficits in understanding and use of gestures; to a total lack of facial expressions and nonverbal communication.

  3. Deficits in developing, maintaining, and understanding relationships, ranging, for example, from difficulties adjusting behavior to suit various social contexts; to difficulties in sharing imaginative play or in making friends; to absence of interest in peers.

Specify **current severity:**

Severity is based on social communication impairments and restricted repetitive patterns of behavior (see Table 2).

B. Restricted, repetitive patterns of behavior, interests, or activities, as manifested by at least two of the following, currently or by history (examples are illustrative, not exhaustive; see text):

  1. Stereotyped or repetitive motor movements, use of objects, or speech (e.g., simple motor stereotypies, lining up toys or flipping objects, echolalia, idiosyncratic phrases).

  2. Insistence on sameness, inflexible adherence to routines, or ritualized patterns of verbal or nonverbal behavior (e.g., extreme distress at small changes, difficulties with transitions, rigid thinking patterns, greeting rituals, need to take same route or eat same food every day).

  3. Highly restricted, fixated interests that are abnormal in intensity or focus (e.g, strong attachment to or preoccupation with unusual objects, excessively circumscribed or perseverative interest).

  4. Hyper- or hyporeactivity to sensory input or unusual interests in sensory aspects of the environment (e.g., apparent indifference to pain/temperature, adverse response to specific sounds or textures, excessive smelling or touching of objects, visual fascination with lights or movement).

Specify **current severity:**

Severity is based on social communication impairments and restricted, repetitive patterns of behavior (see Table 2).

C. Symptoms must be present in the early developmental period (but may not become fully manifest until social demands exceed limited capacities, or may be masked by learned strategies in later life).

D. Symptoms cause clinically significant impairment in social, occupational, or other important areas of current functioning.

E. These disturbances are not better explained by intellectual disability (intellectual developmental disorder) or global developmental delay. Intellectual disability and autism spectrum disorder frequently co-occur; to make comorbid diagnoses of autism spectrum disorder and intellectual disability, social communication should be below that expected for general developmental level.

Note: Individuals with a well-established DSM-IV diagnosis of autistic disorder, Asperger's disorder, or pervasive developmental disorder not otherwise specified should be given the diagnosis of autism spectrum disorder. Individuals who have marked deficits in social communication, but whose symptoms do not otherwise meet criteria for autism spectrum disorder, should be evaluated for social (pragmatic) communication disorder.

Specify **if:**

With or without accompanying intellectual impairment
With or without accompanying language impairment
Associated with a known medical or genetic condition or environmental factor
(**Coding note:** Use additional code to identify the associated medical or genetic condition.)
Associated with another neurodevelopmental, mental, or behavioral disorder
(**Coding note:** Use additional code[s] to identify the associated neurodevelopmental, mental, or behavioral disorder[s].)
With catatonia (refer to the criteria for catatonia associated with another mental disorder, pp. 119-120, for definition) (**Coding note:** Use additional code 293.89 [F06.1] catatonia associated with autism spectrum disorder to indicate the presence of the comorbid catatonia.)

Case Example

SENSORY ISSUES & ASD

Throughout the years, I have encountered numerous individuals with ASD, most with various sensory issues. One child who I worked with for over 10 years was indifferent to pain and temperature. He broke a bone once every year or two years. His parents would never know that he broke a bone until they saw him getting undressed. He was not able to feel the pain of breaking a bone. Several individuals I have seen are overly sensitive to sounds and cover their ears when startled by a sound. Others have had difficulty with certain textures, only eating specific foods that are mushy or crunchy. Many are extremely picky eaters. Others describe being uncomfortable with tags in their clothes or wearing jeans. One young adult told me that brushing her teeth was like brushing with foil. Another young adult described taking a shower as being pelted by sharp nails. I have met other individuals who smell, touch, or eat (e.g., PICA) certain objects over and over again.

Many individuals have a visual fascination with lights or movements. One of the youngest individuals I diagnosed with ASD was a 10-month-old baby girl who was thought to be having seizures. When I consulted with the medical team at the hospital, I put the child on her stomach on the floor. She then tilted her head and began to move her head back-and-forth as she watched the lights flicker around the base of the hospital room floor. It looked as if she was having a seizure since she was quickly moving her head back and forth, but really she was just extremely sensitive to light and began to engage in self-stimulatory behaviors.

One of the most fascinating patients I have worked with was a teenage boy who was diagnosed with ASD, OCD, and selective mutism. He was also gifted with an IQ of 150. I provided therapy to him and his parents for months, although he never talked to me, just shook his head yes or no. He would, however, play chess with me. He was also quite good at chess. After several months of never winning at chess, I made a bet with him. I asked, "If I ever beat you in chess, would you tell me something about yourself?" He got a huge grin (partly because he knew he would never lose) and nodded his head yes. Only once or twice did I mention our bet in the months that passed. I know I didn't need to remind him as he had an amazing memory. One day, I finally beat him (he must have been half asleep). He then told me to look at my computer, which I did immediately. He then asked, "What do you see?" I described whatever was on my computer, some words, a picture, etc. He then commented, "I see pixels." I then asked him if he always saw pixels or was it just on the computer. It seemed that he saw pixels at different times. Since then, I have had other adults with ASD describe that their vision becomes almost impaired or clouded with pixels particularly during unstructured or overly stimulating environments.

OTHER CRITERIA

All symptoms of social communication and restricted repetitive patterns of behavior must be present in the early developmental period and the symptoms must cause clinical functional impairment. In previous versions of the DSM, symptoms were required to be present before the age of three years, which has now changed with the DSM-5. Instead, an individual needs to demonstrate symptoms either currently or by history. The DSM-5 is recognizing that many of these individuals may not display symptoms until they are placed in specific social situations or that some symptoms manifest later in life.

According to the DSM-5, symptoms of ASD may not also be better explained by some other disorder, such as a global developmental delay or intellectual developmental disorder. ASD and an intellectual disability can occur together and if a diagnosis is made, then their social communication symptoms should be below what is expected for their general developmental level. The DSM-5 also noted that if an individual was diagnosed with the DSM-IV with autism, Asperger's disorder, childhood disintegrative disorder, or PDD-NOS, that they will not lose that diagnosis. The only exception to this is if there is an individual who has deficits in social communication but does not have any symptoms related to repetitive or restrictive patterns of interest. These individuals should be reassessed to see if they meet criteria for social pragmatic communication disorder, a new disorder that was added to the DSM-5, which we will discuss again later in this chapter.

The DSM-5 also now allows for specification of other types of accompanying disorders with ASD. This is because many individuals with ASD have other comorbid disorders. For example, some individuals may have

Table 2: Severity Levels For Autism Spectrum Disorder		
Severity Level	**Social Communication**	**Restricted, repetitive behaviors**
Level 3 "**Requiring very substantial support**"	Severe deficits in verbal and nonverbal social communication skills cause severe impairments in functioning, very limited initiation of social interactions, and minimal response to social overtures from others. For example, a person with few words of intelligible speech who rarely initiates interaction and, when he or she does, makes unusual approaches to meet needs only and responds to only very direct social approaches.	Inflexibility of behavior, extreme difficulty coping with change, or other restricted/repetitive behaviors markedly interferes with functioning in all spheres. Great distress/difficulty changing focus or action.
Level 2 "**Requiring substantial support**"	Marked deficits in verbal and nonverbal social communication skills, social impairments apparent even with supports in place; limited initiation of social interactions; and reduced or abnormal responses to social overtures from others. For example, a person who speaks in simple sentences whose interaction is limited to narrow special interests, and who has markedly odd nonverbal communication.	Inflexibility of behavior, difficulty coping with change, or other restricted/repetitive behaviors appear frequently enough to be obvious to the casual observer and interfere with functioning in a variety of contexts. Distress and/or difficulty changing focus or action.
Level 1 "**Requiring support**"	Without supports in place, deficits in social communication cause noticeable impairments. Difficulty initiating social interactions, and clear examples of atypical or unsuccessful responses to social overtures from others. May appear to have decreased interest in social interactions. For example, a person who is able to speak in full sentences and engages in communication but whose to-and-fro conversation with others fails, and whose attempts to make friends are odd and typically unsuccessful.	Inflexibility of behavior causes significant interference with functioning in one or more contexts. Difficulty switching between activities. Problems of organization and planning hamper independence.

Reprinted with permission from the Diagnostic and Statistical Manual of Mental Disorders, Fifth Edition, (Copyright 2013). American Psychiatric Association.

an accompanying intellectual disability, language impairment, a medical or genetic condition, or another type of neurodevelopmental, mental, or behavior disorder.

Another addition to the DSM-5 diagnostic criteria for ASD is the symptom severity level. In the past, many professionals who would diagnose ASD would then describe individuals as mild, moderate, or severe autism. Interesting enough, no professional ever agreed on the definitions of mild, moderate, and severe autism. Professionals were essentially just making up their own definitions. As a result, everyone who would read a report with a diagnosis of mild, moderate, or severe autism would be confused.

In response, the DSM-5 took the initiative to create specific definitions of severity level. They choose not to use the words "mild, moderate, or severe" as these words have been misused in the autism community. Instead they are using level 1, "requiring support," level 2 "requiring substantial support," and level 3 "requiring very substantial support." Now when a qualified professional, such as a developmental pediatrician, neurologist, psychiatrist, or psychologist, diagnoses an individual with ASD, they have the option to specify severity level. It is not required, although it is extremely helpful. In order to diagnose a specific severity level, professionals must take into account symptoms within the communication and restricted repetitive behaviors categories. Each category should received a severity level. For example, an individual can display a level 1 severity level in social communication and a level 2 severity in restricted repetitive behaviors. The more descriptive the evaluator in severity level, the better. It should also be noted that individuals can move from level to level. For example, an individual with ASD at the age of two may be classified as level III, "requiring very substantial support" in social communication, but after receiving intensive interventions for several years, he may move to a level 2, "requiring substantial support" in social communication. Examples of different severity levels are listed in DSM 5 (Table 2).

SOCIAL PRAGMATIC LANGUAGE DISORDER

As mentioned earlier, the DSM-5 added a new diagnosis of social pragmatic language disorder. Social pragmatic language disorder requires the individual to display persistent difficulties in verbal and nonverbal communication

---

■ *Social (Pragmatic) Communication Disorder 315.39 (F80.89)*

Diagnostic Criteria

A. Persistent difficulties in the social use of verbal and nonverbal communication as manifested by all of the following:

1. Deficits in using communication for social purposes, such as greeting and sharing information, in a manner that is appropriate for the social context.

2. Impairment of the ability to change communication to match context or the needs of the listener, such as speaking differently in a classroom than on the playground, talking differently to a child than to an adult, and avoiding use of overly formal language.

3. Difficulties following rules for conversation and storytelling, such as taking turns in conversation, rephrasing when misunderstood, and knowing how to use verbal and nonverbal signals to regulate interaction.

4. Difficulties understanding what is not explicitly stated (e.g., making inferences) and nonliteral or ambiguous meanings of language (e.g., idioms, humor, metaphors, multiple meanings that depend on the context for interpretation).

B. The deficits result in functional limitations in effective communication, social participation, social relationships, academic achievement, or occupational performance, individually or in combination.

C. The onset of the symptoms is in the early developmental period (but deficits may not become fully manifest until social communication demands exceed limited capacities).

D. The symptoms are not attributable to another medical or neurological condition or to low abilities in the domains or word structure and grammar, and are not better explained by autism spectrum disorder, intellectual disability (intellectual developmental disorder), global developmental delay, or another mental disorder.

within social interactions. These individuals do not display any symptoms related to restricted and repetitive behaviors. Individuals who meet criteria for a social pragmatic language disorder diagnosis need to have all of the following symptoms including: 1) deficits in using communication for social purposes, 2) impairment in the ability to change communication to match the context or the needs of the listener, 3) difficulty following rules for conversation and storytelling, and 4) difficulties understanding what is not explicitly stated as well as non-literal or ambiguous meaning of language.

In the past, some individuals who had symptoms of a social pragmatic language disorder may have been diagnosed with pervasive developmental disorder — not otherwise specified. Now we have a separate diagnostic disorder for these individuals. The symptoms must result in clinical functional impairment and also be present in the early developmental period. It should be noted that an individual with ASD cannot also have a separate diagnosis of social pragmatic language disorder. This is because an individual ASD already has deficits in social pragmatic language disorder; therefore, they do not need this additional diagnosis.

Case Example
NIKKI

Nikki is a 10-year-old girl who has a history of difficulty in establishing age-appropriate relationships. Many of her friends are much younger than her and she typically engages in parallel play. She has a passion for playing with toys that are typically for younger children, such as Hello Kitty and Strawberry Shortcake. When greeting others, she is extremely loud, unaware that her voice tone and volume is louder than others. She talks excessively, many times not knowing when a conversation is over or that others have changed the topic of a conversation. Because she has difficulty reading others' social cues, she many times misses when others are teasing her or being sarcastic in conversations. Nikki was previously diagnosed with PDD-NOS, although given that she does not have two behaviors that fall in the repetitive and stereotypical behaviors category in the DSM-5, she now meets criteria for Social (Pragmatic) Communication Disorder.

INTERNATIONAL CLASSIFICATION OF DISEASES AND RELATED HEALTH PROBLEMS (ICD)

When the DSM-5 was first published, individuals with ASD were concerned that they may lose their diagnosis. The DSM-5 has made it clear that if they had that diagnosis before, that they would not lose it, except in the case where they met criteria for a social pragmatic language disorder. With that said, it is important to talk about the other handbook that is used to diagnose mental health disorders. This book is called *International Classification of Diseases and Related Health Problems* (ICD), which is created by the World Health Organization. Typically the ICD manuals have always been published before the latest DSM revision. This is the first time when the DSM has published a revision before the ICD. Currently, those professionals who are billing insurance, which typically includes those individuals who are diagnosing autism, are required to diagnose using the ICD-10. Interestingly, the ICD-10 still allows for the diagnosis of pervasive developmental disorder, childhood autism, atypical autism, Asperger syndrome, other pervasive developmental disorders, and pervasive developmental disorder, unspecified. The diagnostic criteria for childhood autism in the ICD-10 still contain the three symptom areas of reciprocal social interaction, communication, and restricted stereotype repetitive behaviors. Medical and mental health professionals were required by law in 2015 to use the ICD-10 for diagnostic purposes. The ICD-11 is expected to be published in 2018. At this time, we are unsure if the ICD-11 diagnostic criteria for autism will match the DSM-5 criteria. It is hopeful that the diagnostic criteria will be similar given that many professionals who worked on the DSM-5 are also part of the ICD-11 committee for autism disorders. Given it will be up to federal law when professionals are required to begin using the ICD-11, it may take several years before professionals will actually begin using the ICD-11 for billing and diagnostic purposes. Since there are two different diagnostic manuals for autism with numerous revisions, it is recommended for professionals to specify if they are using the DSM-IV, DSM-5, ICD-10, and/or ICD-11 when making their diagnoses.

CONCEPTUAL FRAMEWORK OF AUTISM

The conceptual framework for autism is quite complicated. There are a lot of comorbid disorders that occur with ASD. Comorbid is defined as two or more separate disorders being diagnosed in one individual. Several reviews have indicated that the most comorbid psychiatric conditions with high functioning ASD include AD/HD, Anxiety, Obsessive-Compulsive Disorder, Depression and Bipolar Disorder (Mazzonem, Ruta, & Reale, 2012). Parents report that between 81-87% of children with ASD also were diagnosed with AD/HD, anxiety, behavioral or conduct problems, depression, or developmental delay (Kogan et al., 2007). Given the change in definitions of disorders over time, it is difficult to obtain accurate prevalence rates for several disorders that may be comorbid with ASD. In addition, there may also be a lot of co-occurrence of symptoms that occur across disorders.

As seen in the picture reference below, there are several overlapping neurodevelopmental disorders that may occur with autism. The three fully-colored circles of social impairment, speech communication deficits, and repetitive behaviors and restricted interests are the three symptom categories in the DSM-IV and ICD-10 for ASD. Individuals with ASD sometimes may also be diagnosed with one or more of the other five neurodevelopmental disorders, such as motor disorders, intellectual disabilities, language disorders, specific learning disorders, and AD/HD. Also, there are other disorders that may be comorbid with autism. Particularly, you may see disruptive, impulse control, and conduct disorders, anxiety disorders, or obsessive compulsive and related disorders.

Conceptual Framework

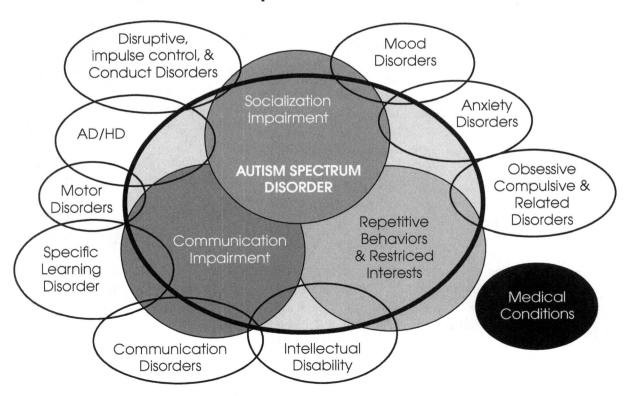

COMORBID DISORDERS

Motor disorders

Motor disorders, such as a developmental coordination disorder or a tic disorder (e.g., Tourette's Disorder or other tic disorder) may also be present in children with ASD. If a child has coordinated motor skills that are substantially below what is expected for their age (e.g., clumsiness, slowness and inaccuracy of fine or gross motor skills, dyspraxia) and it significantly interferes with activities of daily living, then they may have an additional diagnosis of a developmental coordination disorder. About 5-6% of children, ages 5-11 years of age, have minor neurologic dysfunctions. Approximately 75% of children with ASD are also thought to have neurologic dysfunctions. These dysfunctions include impaired posture and muscle tone, fine manipulative disability, mild abnormalities in coordination, and excessive associated movements (Duchan & Patel, 2012).

Tic disorders may also be present. Tourette's Disorder occurs when both motor and vocal tics are present for at least 12 months in a child before the age of 18. The prevalence of Tourette's Disorder in school-age children ranges from 4 to 8 per 1,000 (American Psychiatric Association, 2013). One study reports that the prevalence of Tourette's Disorder in ASD is approximately 6.5% (Zafeiriou, Ververi, & Vargiami, 2007). Another tic disorder is a persistent motor or vocal tick disorder, which occurs when the child only has either a motor or vocal tic that has been present for more than 12 months before the age of 18, whereas a provisional tic disorder occurs when a single or multiple motor and/or vocal tic has been present for less than 12 months.

Intellectual disability

In the United States, it is estimated that approximately 38% of children with ASD also have an intellectual disability (Rice, 2009). To have a diagnosis of an intellectual disability, an individual must have deficits in both intellectual and adaptive functioning with an onset occurring in the developmental period. For intellectual functioning, individuals typically need to have cognitive scores that are approximately two standard deviations or more below the population mean, including a margin for measurement error (e.g., IQ scores below 65-75). Deficits in adaptive functioning describe how an individual is able to function within three domains: 1) conceptual (e.g., skills in language, reading, writing, math, reasoning, knowledge, and memory), 2) social (e.g., empathy, social judgment, interpersonal communication skills, the ability to make and retain friendships), and 3) practical domains (e.g., self-management in areas such as personal care, job responsibilities, money management, recreation, and organizing school and work tasks). Severity levels for intellectual disability (e.g., mild, moderate, severe, or profound) are now based on adaptive functioning, and not IQ scores, as adaptive functioning typically determines the level of support needed.

Communication disorders

Certain communication disorders, such as a language disorder, speech sound disorder, or childhood-onset fluency disorder (e.g. stuttering) may also occur in ASD. A language disorder is the most comorbid of the communication disorders with ASD. According to the DSM-5, a language disorder occurs in the early developmental period and includes the persistent difficulties in the acquisition and use of language (e.g., spoken, written, sign language, etc.) due to deficits in comprehension or production, which includes reduced vocabulary, limited sentence structure, and impairments in discourse that is significantly below what is expected for the child's age.

Specific learning disorder

A specific learning disorder may also occur in combination with ASD. To be diagnosed with a specific learning disability, a child must demonstrate difficulties (e.g., significantly below child's chronological age) in learning and using academic skills that have persisted for at least 6 months despite interventions. The DSM-5 lists six possible symptoms, which a child must have symptoms of one for a specific learning disorder: 1) inaccurate or slow and effortful word reading, 2) difficulty understanding the meaning of what is said, 3) difficulties with spelling, 4) difficulties with written expression, 5) difficulties mastering number sense, number facts, or calculation, and 6) difficulties with mathematical reasoning. Then an impairment in either reading, written expression, or mathematics is specified including severity level (e.g., mild, moderate, or severe).

AD/HD

It's important to discuss AD/HD. A recent review of the literature reports that 33-37% of individuals with ASD also have AD/HD (Berenguer-Forner et al., 2015). There are three different types of AD/HD. First, there is AD/HD predominantly inattentive presentation, sometimes referred to as "ADD." These are individuals who may often fail to pay close attention to details, make careless mistakes, have trouble paying attention, have difficulty following multiple step directions, have trouble organizing tasks, are distracted, and maybe forgetful. The next type of AD/HD is the predominantly hyperactive impulsive presentation. These are individuals who often fidget, can't sit still, talk excessively, say things without thinking, have trouble waiting their turn, and may interrupt others. The last type of AD/HD is the combined type, which are individuals who demonstrate both symptoms of inattention and hyperactivity impulsivity.

Previously, in the DSM-IV, it was presumed that individuals with autism already displayed symptoms of AD/HD; therefore, no separate diagnosis of AD/HD was necessary. Given there are three different types of AD/HD, it is important to identify which type of AD/HD symptoms the individual with ASD may have. Therefore, according to the DSM-5, professionals can diagnose both autism and AD/HD. Based on current research, many individuals with ASD demonstrate executive functioning deficits, which cause symptoms that usually meet criteria for AD/HD inattentive presentation.

Disruptive, impulse control, and conduct disorders

According to the above conceptual framework, there is a very small percent of individuals with ASD who also meet criteria for any type of disruptive, impulse control, or conduct disorder. Unfortunately, many individuals have histories of being misdiagnosed with other disorders before receiving an accurate diagnosis of ASD. Many individuals previously may have been diagnosed with an anxiety disorder, AD/HD, obsessive compulsive disorder (OCD), and/or oppositional defined disorder (ODD). Then, after several years, they find a professional who is qualified to make an autism diagnosis and they receive a diagnosis of ASD. Unfortunately, many of those previous diagnoses continue to follow the individual with ASD throughout their lives (e.g., medical records, reports, etc.). When the individual with ASD presents in a new environment, they may appear to be noncompliant, defiant, and actively annoying others. Individuals may then assume these behaviors are related to a history of oppositional

---

Case Example
JOE

Joe is a verbal two-year-old boy who came to my office for treatment. His parents described him as noncompliant and aggressive at home. He was also obsessed with certain toys and subjects, such as dogs and action figures. When I first saw him, he began to throw toys at my head. He did this for three months. During this time, I attempted to teach him a more appropriate play behavior, such as asking me to play ball (something that still required throwing an object). After three months of not making much progress, I recommended to the family that he receive a comprehensive evaluation. Also, during this time, the mother had another baby. After the baby was born, Joe became more defiant. He began to smear feces on the walls and would try to hurt the baby by putting his thumbs in the baby's eyes. After the comprehensive evaluation, he was diagnosed with pdd-nos, AD/HD, and ODD. Fast forward a couple years and this child in elementary school continued to become more defiant and more aggressive. He would purposefully ruin games he would be playing with his siblings and break their toys. When he was defiant, he was also very manipulative. He would have a thought out plan as to how he would annoy somebody. Many times, when he did annoy someone, he would smile and enjoy the attention he got from it. When he entered middle school, he began to steal items from grocery stores, he would spy on the teachers in the women's restroom, purposely hurt animals, and he began bringing knives and other dangerous weapons to school. As a result, an additional diagnosis of conduct disorder was added.

defiant disorder. Most individuals with ASD may appear to have symptoms of oppositional defined disorder, but in fact, they do not actually have the diagnosis. An individual with oppositional defined disorder is wired differently than an individual with ASD. The brain development of an individual with oppositional defiant disorder is different than the brain development of an individual with ASD. With that said, there are a small number of individuals with ASD who also have oppositional defiant disorder, but this occurs less frequently.

An individual who truly has oppositional defiant disorder may later receive a diagnosis of conduct disorder or antisocial personality disorder. Most individuals with ASD are not wired to hurt people. They are not wired to annoy people. They do not come up with a specific plan to annoy people. Because they have ASD, they become rigid and focused on specific routines. When their routine is disrupted, they can become aggressive, defiant, and noncompliant. These behaviors are a result of the routine being disrupted, not the result of a diagnosis of oppositional defiant disorder. This is important to remember when professionals are working with an individual with ASD who has a previous diagnosis of ODD. This history of a diagnosis of ODD may have been inappropriately given based on only a clinical interview and not a comprehensive evaluation. If this is the case, a comprehensive evaluation should be conducted to determine if the individual actually has ODD.

Anxiety disorders

Various anxiety disorders have been frequently observed in individuals with ASD, including generalized anxiety disorder, separation anxiety, specific phobias, and social phobias. Prevalence rates are inconsistent, due to differences in research methodology, although comorbidity of anxiety with ASD is well-documented (Matson & Nebel-Schwalm, 2007). Many times, anxiety is easier to diagnosis in high functioning and/or older individuals. In addition, these individuals typically respond better to cognitive-behavioral therapy to reduce symptoms. Furthermore, it is apparent that symptoms of anxiety co-occur many times with ASD as many individuals with ASD report intense feelings of anxiety particularly during overly stimulated activities and unstructured environmental settings.

Mood disorders

Some individuals with ASD may also experience a mood disorder, such as depression or even bipolar disorder, at some point in their lives. A review of studies shows prevalence of mood disorders to be higher in older individuals with ASD, although this also may be due to a lack of reliable measures to diagnosis mood disorders in children (Matson & Nebel-Schwalm, 2007). It is important to identify mood disorders in individuals with ASD, as a comorbid diagnosis may negatively impact long-term goals and lead to withdrawal, non-compliance, aggression, or even suicide.

Obsessive compulsive and related disorders

Some individuals with ASD may also have Obsessive-Compulsive Disorder (OCD). OCD in an individual with ASD looks very different. Most individuals with ASD will perseverate on a certain

---

Case Example

AARON

Aaron is a 10-year-old boy with ASD and OCD. Aaron talks excessively and verbally checks with others about his schedule. He has a very difficult time focusing on the present. A two card visual system was used with Aaron. One card said "work" and one card said "play." After his work, the play card would be put at the top of his schedule and the work card would be moved down on his schedule. Aaron would then quickly say repeatedly while rocking, "It's time to play now. It's time to play. It's time to play now, right? Dr. Daily, it's time to play now. But I have to work next. I have to work next. I have to work next. Work is next, right Dr. Daily?" Aaron was so worried about what he had to do next that he had to constantly check and ask questions to relieve the anxiety. For Aaron, it is better just to present one visual card of what he should be focusing on now so that he is not worried about what is next on his schedule.

---

subject, interest, or object, but they do not engage in symptoms of OCD. To have a diagnosis of OCD, one must have obsessions (e.g., recurrent and persistent thoughts, urges or images that are intrusive and unwanted, which the individual attempts to ignore or suppress) as well compulsions (e.g., repetitive behaviors that the individual feels driven to perform that are aimed at preventing or reducing anxiety or some dreaded event).

Medical conditions

Lastly on the ASD conceptual framework, it is important to notice that there are also medical conditions or symptoms, such as sleep problems, immune and gastrointestinal dysfunction, as well as possible seizures and EEG differences that many times occur with ASD (Treating Autism and Autism Treatment Trust, 2013). Most individuals with ASD have sleep problems related to their perseverations or anxiety. This may be because they have AD/HD combined type or hyperactive-impulsive type so that they have more energy, or they have an unbalanced life style such as poor eating, sleeping, and exercise habits. EEG differences are also quite common with ASD as well as sometimes seizures. Many individuals may also have immune or gastrointestinal issues, which is why it is always important to have a multidisciplinary team of medical professionals assessing the individual.

Chapter TWO

Etiology and Brain Development

PREVALENCE AND ETIOLOGY

The prevalence rates for ASD are always changing. Recently the Centers for Disease Control and Prevention (Boyle et al., 2011; Baio, 2012; Developmental, 2014) stated that one in every six children are diagnosed with a neurodevelopmental disorder, which would include ASD, AD/HD, motor disorders, intellectual disabilities, language disorders, and specific learning disorders. At this time, one in every 68 children are diagnosed with autism. ASD is growing at a rate of 30% and is five times more common in boys than girls. We know that it is a biologically-based neurodevelopmental disorder. Etiology is still not clear, although there are some genetic and environmental factors that are promising in the research.

Genetics

Numerous studies demonstrate a strong relationship between ASD and genetics. ASD is highly heritable. Even in older studies conducted in the 1990s, there is a 70-80% concordance rate in monozygotic or identical twins using a very strict definition of autism (Baily and colleagues, 1995; Lichtenstein et al., 2010). When the phenotype or definition of autism is broadened to include all pervasive developmental disorders (e.g., autism, Asperger's Disorder, PDD-NOS), there is approximately an 85-90% concordance rate in monozygotic twins (Baily and colleagues, 1995; Lichtenstein et al., 2010). The rate of autism among siblings of a child with ASD is greater than the typical population. Those statistics range from 2 to 18% (Rutter, 1999; Ozonoff and colleagues, 2011), with siblings being 25 times more likely to have autism (Abrahams & Geschwind, 2008; Geschwind, 2009). There is also a plethora of research on specific genes that may be associated with ASD (Muhle and colleagues, 2004, Miles, 2011), although few of the genes are specific to ASD. Many of the specific genes being studied for ASD may also contribute to the genetic risk for other disorders such as intellectual disability, schizophrenia, specific learning disability, epilepsy and ADHD (Geschwind, 2011).

Fewer than 10 to 15% of individuals with ASD are also associated with another medical condition, genetic disorder, or known syndrome including Fragile X, Neurocutaneous disorders, PKU, Prader-Willi, Fetal Alcohol Syndrome, Angelman Syndrome, Rett Syndrome, Smith-Lemli-Opitz syndrome (Johnson & Myers, 2007). Because of these statistics, the American Academy of Pediatrics recommends that any individual diagnosed with ASD should receive genetic testing. In addition, any siblings of an individual with ASD should also be screened for ASD.

Environmental factors

In several studies, we have seen correlations with some environmental factors. It should be noted that these are correlations and do not conclude a cause and effect relationship. Several studies have demonstrated that ASD is correlated with maternal and/or paternal age (Croen and colleagues, 2007; Kolevzon and colleagues, 2007). Over the age of 35, the risk of having a child with ASD increases significantly. Also, maternal diabetes is a significant risk factor during pregnancy (Xu, 2013). Other studies have demonstrated some teratogens or environment factors in the first trimester of pregnancy that are correlated with an increased risk of ASD. For example, some studies have demonstrated first trimester exposure to maternal rubella infection, ethanol, thalidomide, valproic acid, and misoprostol as a correlation with ASD (Arndt, Strodgell, & Rodier, 2005).

DIFFERENCE IN BRAIN DEVELOPMENT

Environment factors, such as prenatal teratogens, and genetics play a role in the brain's development of any infant. Autism is no different. Over the past five years, there has been substantial research focusing on brain development of individuals with ASD.

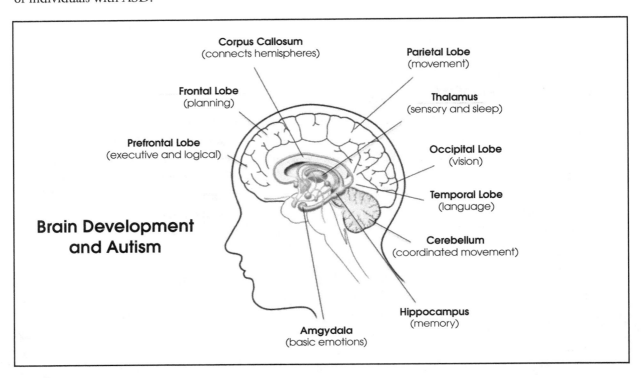

First, there have been numerous studies that have demonstrated differences in the brain's electrical activity of an individual with ASD compared to a typical individual (Amaral, Schumann, & Nordahl, 2008). Certain studies have showed differences in the corpus callosum (Alexander et al., 2007; Catani et al., 2008), which is responsible for the communication between the right and left hemisphere and the amgydala, which is responsible for basic emotions (Schumann, 2004; Schumann & Amaral, 2006). A more recent study with a large sample size was able to replicate several other studies indicating differences in the cerebellum, which is responsible for coordinated movement, the thalamus, which processes most sensory information (except olfactory) and helps regulate sleep, the hippocampus, which is responsible for memory, and the globus pallidus, which is part of the basal ganglia and regulates voluntary movement (Sussman et al., 2015). Other studies have also demonstrated that there are neurons that are specifically disrupted in the temporal lobe (Pelphrey and colleagues, 2011), which is associated with processing sensory input to understand visual memories, language comprehension, and emotions. In addition, there appears to also be an excess of neurons in the prefrontal cortex (Courchesne et al., 2011), which is associated with executive functioning, such as planning and decision-making, and moderating social behavior. Often those studies have demonstrated that the brain of an individual with ASD sometimes has abnormal formation of synapses and dendritic spines compared to the brain of a typical individual (Persico & Bourgeron, 2006).

Furthermore, there are differences in some of the neurotransmitters in the brain of an individual with ASD, specifically differences in serotonin (Levy, Mandell, & Schultz, 2009), which is thought to contribute to mood, as well as glutamate (Mariani et al., 2015), particularly in Fragile X (Dolen and colleagues, 2007), which plays a role in neuron activity. The excess of neurons in the brain of an individual with ASD can sometimes cause over connectivity (Courchesne and colleagues, 2007) or it can cause under connectivity (Just and colleagues, 2007) in certain parts of the brain (Pelphrey and colleagues, 2011). A recent study by Danjani and Uddin (2015) demonstrated that individuals with ASD demonstrated lower connectivity in sensory processing parts of the brain and higher connectivity in the complex information processing part of the brain. Those with higher connectivity in ASD also demonstrated more severe ASD symptoms. Additionally, the differences in the over and under connectivity were more pronounced in childhood than adulthood.

Researchers have also found disturbed neuronal migration that occurs early during the gestational phase of development (Schmitz & Rezaie, 2008; Persico & Bourgeron, 2006). In addition, individuals with ASD have shown significant overgrowth of the brain (Courchesne, Carper & Ashoomoff, 2003; Courchesnes, Piere, & Schumann, 2007; Hazlett, Poe, & Gerig, 2005), particularly males, and their lobe-based cortical thickness does not appear to decrease in thickness between childhood and adolescence, which is demonstrated by typical peers (Sussman et al., 2015).

Several neuropsychologists have focused on the mirror neuron system. The mirror neuron system stems from theory of mind or the difficulty that individuals with ASD have in taking on the other person's perspective. In the studies, both individuals with ASD and typical individuals are monitored through fMRIs that measure the brains electrical activity. Individuals are asked to perform a specific task, such as imitating emotional expressions, and the brains electrical activity would be measured during this task. Then the same individuals would be asked to observe another individual engaging in that same task of imitating emotional expressions while measuring their brains electrical activity. fMRIs conducted on typical individuals show neurons firing in specific areas of the brain when they engaged in the task as well as when they observed someone engage in that exact task. In comparison, an individual with ASD would demonstrate neurons firing when completing the task but when they observed someone else doing that same task, the neurons were not firing in that part of the brain (the inferior frontal gyrus). Thus the studies concluded that individuals with ASD may have a dysfunctional mirror neuron system (Dapretto et al., 2006; Iacoboni & Dapretto, 2006).

Several studies have shown how individuals with ASD have difficulty integrating or processing information from multiple senses (Russo and colleagues, 2010; Bradwein et al., 2013; Marco et al., 2011). Some researchers have found that individuals with ASD have a delayed response to certain auditory signals (Russo et al., 2009; Kwakye et al., 2010). When studying visual processing, it appears that individuals with ASD have atypical peripheral visual processing, concluding that they are better able to see one specific point in their vision, but when asked to view items in their peripheral vision, they have more difficulty (Frey and colleagues, 2013). Furthermore, it has been long studied that individuals with ASD have difficulties directing their gaze to socially relevant stimuli such as faces and eyes, which leads to difficulties in facial recognition (Pelphrey et al., 2002; Hernadez et al., 2009; Kliemann et al., 2010).

Other studies have focused on measuring brain activity using fMRIs while having individuals with ASD perform specific tasks. In a study of visual working memory, typical individuals processed the visual memory tasks in a verbally oriented style, using verbal-phonological codes, activating the left-hemisphere language and frontal working memory brain areas (e.g., left parietal and prefrontal regions), which are associated with verbal tasks. In comparison, individuals with ASD processed the visual memory task in a more nonverbal and visually oriented processing style, using visual-graphical codes, activating the right-hemisphere visuo-graphic brain regions (e.g., right parietal and frontal regions) (Koshino et al., 2005). Similarly, another study, which focused on auditory comprehension, found that individuals with ASD processed the information in the parietal and occipital parts of the brain, using visual imagery or thinking in pictures, when the task did not require it (Kana et al., 2006). High functioning adults with ASD have many times reported that when they hear others talk they visualize step-by-step pictures in their brain. This research may support this theory.

So what does all this research mean for treating and educating individuals with ASD? Several comprehensive studies, focused on the neuropsychological functioning of individuals with ASD compared to typical peers, have created a profile of intact and impaired abilities (Minshew, Goldstein, & Siegel, 1997; Williams, Goldstein, & Minshew, 2006, Williams & Minshew, 2010).

INTACT ABILITIES

Basic attention

Studies indicate that the individual with ASD can engage in basic attention. It is important to understand the definition of basic attention. Basic attention is defined as the ability to attend to one thing at a time. For example, if I had four items on my desk, such as a phone, a pencil, a piece of paper, and an eraser, an individual with ASD would only be able to attend to one item at a time. So if he or she was attending to the pencil, that individual with ASD would not be able to attend to the phone, paper, or eraser.

Elementary motor

Based on this research, most individuals with ASD have intact elementary motor skills. Elementary motor is defined as performing one motor skill at a time. If they have any other impairments in motor abilities, this would likely be related to a separate motor disorder.

Sensory perception

Brain development studies of ASD demonstrate that those individuals with ASD have intact or enhanced abilities in sensory perception. Each individual with ASD is different. Some individuals with ASD may be more sensitive to sounds than lights. Other individuals may be more sensitive to touch than smells. The sensitivity is based on the electrical activity and specific neuron differences in each individual's brain.

Simple memory

The research demonstrates that individuals with ASD have an intact or even enhanced simple memory. It is important to not confuse simple memory with complex memory. Simple memory can be detailed memory. For example, if I was to ask an individual with ASD who has never received any type of intervention to tell me about their day, they might then tell me every specific detail. For instance, they might say, "My alarm went off at 8 AM and I leaned over to shut my alarm off and then I heard my German Shepherd bark so I walked down the stairs and open the back door to let the dog out to go to the bathroom. I then filled the dog's dish with kibbles and bits and then went to the bathroom to wash my hands." They might continue to tell me every detail of what happened that day. That is called simple detailed memory, meaning they are attending to one piece of information at a time.

Formal language

Based on brain development research, we also know that the formal language aspects in the brain of ASD, such as the phonological and grammatical elements of communication, are in fact intact and for some may be enhanced. If an individual with ASD is demonstrating other communication impairments such as articulation delays or an expressive or receptive language delay, this would be considered a communication disorder that is not related to ASD.

Rule-learning

In the brain of an individual with ASD, the research demonstrates that the rule learning aspects of the brain are intact or enhanced. This is typically why individuals with ASD are extremely focused on schedules or rules. When a schedule or rule is changed or not being followed, the part of the brain that allows them to be flexible is impaired.

Visuospatial processing

Most individuals with ASD have intact or enhanced abilities in visual spatial processing. They are not only visualizing what they hear, but they are processing information visually and spatially. Visual information is their primary language.

IMPAIRED ABILITIES

Executive functioning

Many individuals with ASD have an impairment in the temporal and prefrontal cortex, which is responsible for executive functioning. This higher-level cognitive functioning may include difficulties with inhibition, flexible thinking, problem-solving, planning, impulse control, concept formation, abstract thinking and creativity.

Integrative processing

Any type of integrative or complex processing may be impaired. For example, any type of complex sensory, motor, memory, or language skills are going to be difficult for an individual with ASD. This is because they are only able to attend to one skill or piece of information at a time.

Visuospatial facial recognition

Several studies have demonstrated that individuals with ASD have difficulties with facial recognition. Individuals with ASD, if they are only able to attend to one piece of information at a time, have difficulty processing someone's face. They may only be able to attend to the individual's nose or mouth. Given that typical individuals use their entire face to express emotions, individuals with ASD have difficulty understanding that emotion if they can only attend to one part of the individual's face. In fact, if you ask adults with ASD how they recognize another person, they will typically tell you they recognize others by their hairstyle or their skin tone. They have a very difficult time recognizing another individual by their face.

Concept formation

Concept or prototype formation is the ability to organize information into different categories. Jean Piaget (1952), a well-known developmental psychologist, redefined this as a schema. For example, a typical developing child at the age of two may see a poodle, cocker spaniel, and shih tzu, and call all of them "dog." In comparison, an individual with ASD might say, "That is a poodle, a cocker spaniel, and a shih tzu." The ability to create the concept of "dog" for all three of the breeds does not work the same way in their brain. I had one adult with ASD tell me that they did not understand the concept of "no" growing up. They thought "no" meant "no, never, forever." "No" seems like a fairly concrete concept, but in our everyday language it is quite abstract. If a child asks a parent, "Can I play a video game?" and the parent says, "No, we are going to your grandmother's house," the child with ASD would likely start to tantrum, assuming they were never able to play the video game ever again. The parent may have just meant they could play the game later.

Auditory processing

Based on the research on brain development with individuals with ASD, we now understand that they are different in how they process human speech and how they integrate complex occipital lobe, auditory information. Many individuals with ASD appear to process auditory information in the right hemisphere instead of the left hemisphere, occipital lobe, which means they are processing auditory information visually. We have known for years that intervention such as the picture exchange communication system (PECs) has been helpful in teaching individuals with ASD. Given this latest research, this makes sense. If an individual's primary language is visual, then it would be helpful for us to talk less and use more visuals.

CHAPTER THREE

The Key to Autism

INFORMATION PROCESSING MODEL

Typical individuals process information based on the environmental information that they receive with all five senses. They attend to that information which transfers to their working memory, which either they encode into long-term memory to retrieve it when needed or they rehearse it in their working memory and respond. Now, individuals with ASD are going to process information differently based on the research. Even in conversations with adults with ASD, many report that they only attend to one basic piece of information at a time, particularly when they are stressed or are processing too much sensory information. If they are only able to attend to one thing at a time, then they are only able to attend to one piece of information that they are processing from their senses. So, instead of understanding the environment from all five senses, they may only be attending to what they hear. If they are hypersensitive to sound, then many times they may be attending to things that they do not like and that is what is going into the working memory that either gets encoded into long-term memory or they rehearse it in working memory and that is what they respond to. This model explains why many times individuals with ASD misunderstand the contextual situation. If they are only able to process one piece of information at a time and they attend to a piece of information that is either not relevant or a minor piece of information in the larger contextual environment, then they are really not able to process the information properly.

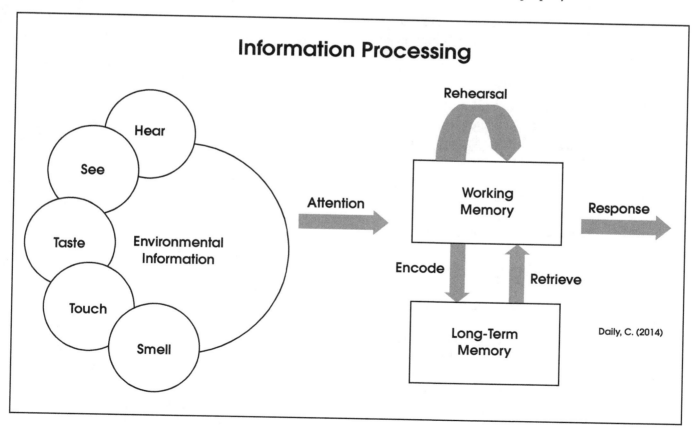

Information Processing

Daily, C. (2014)

THE KEY ANALOGY

To help professionals and caregivers better understand autism, I've created a key analogy based on brain development research and information processing as well as reports from adults with ASD. If an individual with ASD is presented with a task, he or she has a set of keys for that task. Each key is a specific step or one piece of information that is needed to complete that task.

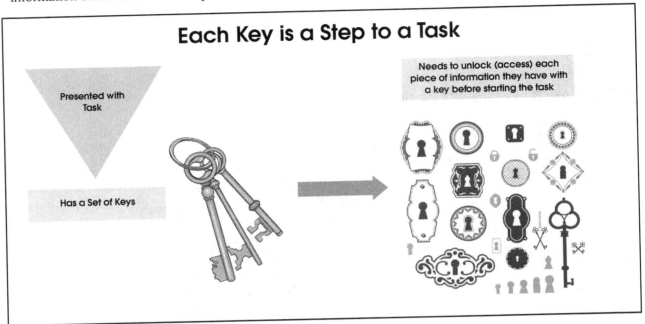

For example, if I asked an individual with ASD to brush his teeth, that individual would have a key for walking into the bathroom, a key for getting out his toothbrush, a key for getting the toothpaste, a key for taking the lid off the toothpaste, a key for setting the lid down, a key for squirting the toothpaste onto the toothbrush, and so forth. That individual is visually picturing each step required to brush his teeth before he even steps into the bathroom to brush his teeth. It's like he has to unlock each lock on the door with a key before even walking through the door.

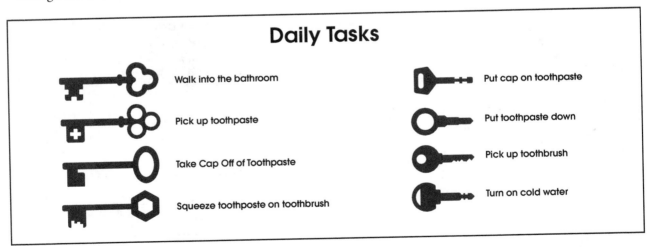

How often are you presented with a task in a quiet non-disruptive environment? For an individual with ASD who may be hyper or hypo sensitive to certain environmental or sensory stimuli, they are constantly disrupted. Also, as a society, we expect tasks to be done quickly. Many times we forget that an individual with ASD processes auditory information at a much slower rate than the typical individual not to mention they are visualizing the information. When talking with a person with ASD, I constantly have to remind myself to stop and allow them to take the time needed to respond or to ask a clarifying question. If I start to say something because they didn't answer a question quickly, I have essentially interrupted their thought process. The same is true in this key analogy. If an individual is presented with a task to go brush his teeth, then two minutes later, the parent may see the child still standing in the hallway looking as if he is doing nothing. In reality, he may be processing and visualizing each step that is required to brush his teeth. Without realizing, often the parent then yells at him, "Why are you not brushing your teeth?"

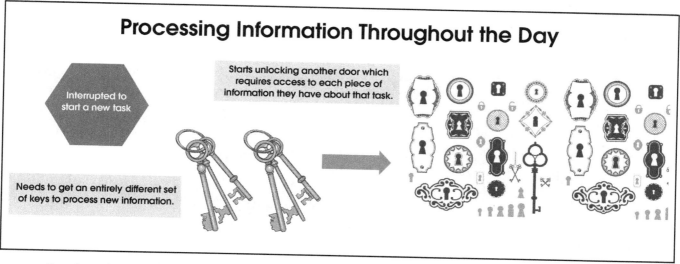

Processing Information Throughout the Day

Interrupted to start a new task

Starts unlocking another door which requires access to each piece of information they have about that task.

Needs to get an entirely different set of keys to process new information.

Based on this analogy, once interrupted, the child then has to restart the entire process of visualizing each step of the task again. If he is given another task in addition to the first task, then he is going to need to get a new set of different keys to process that new information. He then starts unlocking another door which requires access to each piece of information that they have about that task. For only an hour, I want you to imagine all the unfinished tasks that an individual with ASD may not have completed because they are not given enough time to process and complete that task with interruptions. It would be extremely frustrating.

End of the Day

Several years ago, I had the privilege of listening to Dr. Steven Shore present on autism. Dr. Shore himself has acknowledged that he has some tendencies of an individual with ASD. During this conference, Dr. Shore had asked us to get into small groups as he wanted us to understand what it is like to have ASD. This was one of the best, yet most uncomfortable activities I have ever experienced. It was a great learning tool for me. As such, I have adapted his activity for others to use to better understand autism. This activity only works for groups of four or five individuals. The group activity is performed in the following manner:

A DAY IN THEIR SHOES

Directions: First, assign each person into a group by numbering off from 1 to 4 (or 5). Give each person in the group one of the following 5 tasks:

1. Sit in the chair as the identified person with autism.

2. Stand behind #1 and move the edge of a paper up and down the back of the neck of #1.

3. Stand next to #1 and hums/sings a song into #1's ear.

4. Stand on the other side of #1 and talks to #1 about what he/she ate for breakfast and what it tasted and smelled like. If you do this around lunch time, they could even place food in front of #1 to activate their sense of smell and taste.

5. Stand in front of #1 and claps their hands repeatedly in front of #1's eyes. If there is a group of four, then #1 also has the roll of #5 and should clap their hands in front of their own eyes.

It is important to do this activity 4 or 5 times so that each person has the opportunity to be the identified person with autism. Once everyone knows their role, then tell the group that you will be teaching them something and they will need to answer questions after the activity. Then have everyone get into their groups. Some groups will be far away from the presenter and some may be closer to the presenter, which is ok.

Once they are in their groups, tell them to start. Then read one of the vignettes below. After reading a vignette, tell them to stop. When they stop, ask only those individuals who were identified as #1 to answer the questions listed below that vignette. Almost everyone will not be able to answer. After that, have everyone switch places (e.g., #1 is now #2, #2 is now #3, #3 is now #4, #4 is now #5, #5 is now #1) and then continue on with the activity until everyone has had a chance to be #1.

VIGNETTES

1. Brandon is in the 5th grade at Green Elementary School. He went to the doctor's office on Thursday after school because his stomach hurt. Brandon's mother kept him home from school the next day.
   a. What grade is Brandon in?
   b. What day did Brandon miss school?

2. Maria is four years old. She is celebrating her birthday next week on Friday. She is planning to have a big pool party on Sunday.
   a. What day of the week is Maria's birthday?
   b. How old will she be?

3. Kate stayed after school on Monday to help her science teacher clean the classroom. Her favorite class is Social Studies. She has a test in English tomorrow.
   a. What is Kate's favorite class?
   b. What day is her English test?

4. Lucy's mom packed a lunch for Lucy at school on Wednesday. She had a ham sandwich and chips. The day before she got to buy a lunch, which was pizza.
    a. What kind of sandwich did Lucy eat?
    b. What day did she have pizza?

5. Robert is planning a vacation for his mother to go to Florida in April. The month after that he has to travel to New York for work.
    a. Who is going on vacation?
    b. What month he is traveling to New York?

It is best to process this activity after everyone has had a chance to participate as those who are number 1 typically want to share the experience right away. Participants will discover multiple things. Some possible discussion questions include:

1. How did it feel to be number 1?

2. What sensory stimuli did you attend to the most?

3. What sensory input bothered you the most?

4. What sensory input did you like the most?

5. How did you cope?

6. What information were you able to understand?

Note: Many times, participants will say that they felt anxious, frustrated, annoyed, and/or angry. Each participant will attend to a different sensory stimuli depending upon each individual's preference. Sometimes participants will cope by shutting down, closing their eyes, looking at something on the floor or wall, attempting to make eye contact with the presenter, or even engaging in self-stimulatory behaviors. After the first couple examples, participants will begin to be able to answer the more concrete questions, such as Kate's favorite class or what Lucy's mom packed for lunch. They typically have more difficulty answering questions that require more complex understanding of information that requires more than one piece of information, such as the day of Kate's English test or what day Lucy had pizza. Typically, the only participants who are able to answer those questions are the participants who are within an arm's length away from the presenter and usually sitting at a 90-degree angle from the presenter. You can do several versions of this activity to demonstrate other points, such as presenting the vignettes visually instead of auditorily. Most everyone will be able to answer the follow up questions when the information is presented visually.

Chapter FOUR

Screening and Assessment

SCREENING

The American Academy of Pediatrics recommends autism screenings for every child at 9, 18 and 24 (or 30) months, since signs of autism can be detected as early as 18 months of age. The Counsel for Children with Disabilities and the American Academy of Pediatrics (Johnson, Myers, 2007) recommend screening a child for ASD if any of the following are present:

- Lack of appropriate gaze
- Lack of recognition of parent voice
- Decrease or absent use of prespeech gestures (e.g., pointing, waving, showing)
- Lack of warm, joyful expressions with gaze
- Lack of response to vocalizations (e.g., name), but very aware of environmental sounds
- Lack of expressions such as "uh oh" or "huh"
- Lack of turn-taking patterns between infant and parent
- Delayed onset of babbling past 9 months
- Lack of interest or response of any kind to neutral statements

Developmental screeners

When screening an individual for ASD, it is important to use a screening tool that is both valid and reliable. There are several general developmental screening tools, such as the **Communication and Symbolic Behavior Scales** (CSBS) by Wetherby and Prizant (2002), the **Ages and Stages Questionnaires** (ASQ-3) by Bricker and Squires (1999; 2009), and the **Parents' Evaluation of Developmental Status** (PEDS) by Glascoe (2010) that may be helpful. The CSBS has the Infant Toddler Checklist (ITC), or CSBS DP™, which screens for early developmental delays in social communication, expressive speech/language, and symbolic functioning for infants 6 months to 24 months of age. The Brookes Publishing Co. website offers this free 24-item parent report checklist. The ASQ-3 is a 30-item parent report questionnaire for children 1 month to 66 months of age that measures communication, fine motor, gross motor, personal-social, and problem-solving skills. The Ages & Stages Questionnaires website provides this questionnaire for free. In comparison, the PEDS is a 10-item parent report questionnaire for children 1 month to eight years of age that reports developmental concerns in the five areas of global/cognitive, expressive language, receptive language, social-emotional, and other.

Autism screeners

In addition to general screeners, there are now some specific screeners that assess risk for autism, sometimes called Level 1 screeners. One of the most widely-used autism screeners to identify risk is the **Modified Checklist for Autism in Toddlers** (MCHAT–R/F), created initially by Diana Robins (2008) and then revised by Robins and colleagues (2014), which is used for children 16 to 30 months of age. **A copy of the MCHAT-R/F is included at the end of this chapter**. The Follow-up portion of the MCHAT-R/F is also recommended for use, particularly for scores in the mid range (total scores of 3-7). Due to the length of the Follow-up portion, it is not included in this chapter, but can be downloaded at the M-CHAT™ website. The MCHAT-R/F has been reported as the strongest Level 1 autism-specific screening tool if the follow-up portion of the measure is also used (Ibanez, Stone, & Coonrod, 2014).

One of the first autism screeners to be created was the **Checklist for Autism in Toddlers**, better known as the CHAT (Baron-Cohen, Allen, & Gillberg, 1992). Originally, it was used to identify 18-month-old infants at risk for autism in the United Kingdom. Now, it is sometimes used at the 18-month developmental pediatrician well-check appointment. It looks at behaviors such as joint attention and pretend play. Nine items are completed by the parent and five items are observations made by the primary care physician. One other screener worth mentioning is the **Early Screening of Autistic Traits Questionnaire or ESAT** (Dietz et al., 2006; Swinkels et al., 2006), which is a 14-item yes/no questionnaire that was developed using a sample of children ages 8 to 20 months olds. (For more information regarding specific screeners and evaluation of ASD, see Johnson, Myers, 2007).

DIAGNOSIS AND ASSESSMENT

Assessment of ASD is a large topic, too challenging to cover in just one chapter of a book. A comprehensive study of all the ins and outs of assessment and ASD is *Assessment of Autism Spectrum Disorders* (Goldstein & Naglieri, 2008). Given the breadth of information on assessment of ASD, the main components of diagnosis and assessment are highlighted.

Diagnosis

Professionals who can diagnose autism are either a neurologist, psychiatrist, psychologist, or developmental pediatrician. When diagnosing ASD, a comprehensive evaluation should be conducted, which would include obtaining full health, developmental and behavioral histories, a complete medical exam, and then evaluating the individual's cognitive, language, social-emotional, behavioral, and adaptive behavior functioning. To receive a diagnosis, the child must meet criteria for ASD in either the DSM-5 or ICD-10.

Assessment team

A multi-disciplinary team is recommended when assessing a child with ASD. This team many times includes a psychologist, speech-language pathologist, occupational therapist, and sometimes other professionals such as a physical therapist, board certified behavior analyst (BCBA), and other team members. Of course, parents and educators should also be included throughout the evaluation process.

Psychologists and neuropsychologists are professionals who typically do comprehensive testing for ASD. Not all psychologists specialize in ASD, thus it is important to find one that has specialized training in ASD assessment. Testing may include cognitive functioning, adaptive behavior functioning, academic functioning, autism spectrum rating scales, play-based assessments, social-emotional scales, and behavior rating scales.

Given many of the social pragmatic language and communication difficulties individuals with ASD possess, it is also important to have a speech-language evaluation. A speech-language pathologist can assess language skills, social competency, phonology, dyspraxia, apraxia, articulation, hearing, voice tone and volume, oral-motor skills, pragmatic language, and verbal fluency.

An evaluation by an occupational therapist is also helpful when diagnosing ASD. According to the American Occupational Therapy Association (2010), for individuals with an ASD, the scope of occupational therapy services across the life course may include regulation of emotional and behavioral responses, processing of sensory information necessary for participation, development of social abilities, interpersonal skills and peer relationships, self-management skills, skills needed for success in school and assistive technology for accomplishing communication, school, or work functions. An occupational therapist can assess a wide variety of skills including:

- Sensory modulation, integrative, defensiveness, registration, and processing difficulties
- Affected gross and fine motor development
- Feeding and Toileting issues
- Postural issues
- Lack of organizational skills
- Visual perception and perceptual motor difficulties
- Poor play skills and socialization

- Auditory discrimination difficulties
- Presence of primitive reflexes
- Motor planning and Bilateral coordination difficulties
- Lack of awareness of body and body position in space
- Poor fine motor skills: e.g., Eye-hand coordination and Handwriting difficulties
- Work behavior issues
- Emotional issues

If gross motor skills (e.g., sitting, walking, running, or jumping) are a concern, then an evaluation by a physical therapist is also recommended. A physical therapist can design activities to treat poor muscle tone, balance, and coordination. In addition, if the child already has a diagnosis of ASD, a BCBA may perform a functional behavioral assessment on specific behaviors or assess specific skill areas using measures such as:

- **Assessment of Basic Skills and Language** – Revised (ABLLS-R; Partington, 2006)
- **Verbal Behavior Milestones Assessment and Placement Program** (VB-MAPP; Sundberg, 2008)
- **Eden Autism Assessment and Curriculum Series** (Eden Autism Services, 2009)

Cognitive functioning

Cognitive or intellectual testing is recommended as part of a comprehensive ASD evaluation (Johnson, Myers, & the Council on Children with Disabilities, 2009). Cognitive testing typically measures the strengths and weaknesses in both verbal and nonverbal abilities in problem solving, concept formation, reasoning, style of learning, memory skills, and other possible domains. The most widely used measures for cognitive functioning that have been standardized on individuals with ASD are:

- **Bayley Scales of Infant and Toddler Development**, Third Edition (Bayley-III; Bayley, 2006)
- **Wechsler Preschool and Primary Scale of Intelligence** – Third Edition (WPPSI-IV; Wechsler, 2012)
- **Wechsler Intelligence Scale for Children** – Fourth Edition (WISC-V; Wechsler, 2014)
- **Woodcock Johnson III Tests of Cognitive Abilities** (WJ-III; Woodcock, McGrew, & Mather, 2001; 2007a; Schrank IV, McGrew & Mather, 2014b)
- **Stanford-Binet Intelligence Scales**, Fifth Edition (SB5; Roid, 2003).

Adaptive functioning

Assessment in adaptive behavior is also recommended for any individual with a possible ASD. As mentioned earlier, adaptive functioning includes how an individual is able to function within conceptual, social, and practical domains. Widely-used adaptive functioning measures that have been standardized in individuals with ASD:

- **Vineland Adaptive Behaviors Scales** – Second Edition (Sparrow et al., 2005)

- **Adaptive Behavior Assessment System** – Second Edition (ABAS-II; Harrison & Oakland, 2003)

Autism scales

There are several scales, including rating scales, interviews, and observational assessments that measure specific symptoms related to ASD. The most commonly used rating scales include:

- **Childhood Autism Rating Scales**, Second Edition (CARS2; Schopler, Bourgondien, Wellman, & Love, 2010)

- **Gilliam Autism Rating Scale** – Third Edition (GARS-3; Gilliam, 2013)

The Autism Diagnostic Interview – Revised (ADI-R; Lord, Rutter, & Le Couteur, 1994) is a semi-structured interview with the parent or caregiver that requires extensive training to administer and, therefore, is many times used primarily for research. Currently, one of the most widely-used assessment measures is the **Autism Diagnostic Observation Schedule**, Second Edition (ADOS-2; Lord, Luyster, Gotham & Guthrie, 2012; Lord, Rutter, Risi, Gotham, & Bishop, 2012), which is a standardized observational assessment that measures social affect (e.g., communication and reciprocal social interactions) and restricted and repetitive behaviors.

Academic functioning

Sometimes achievement measures are given to evaluate an individual's academic functioning. The most common achievement tests given to individuals with ASD are:

- **Woodcock Johnson IV Tests of Achievement** (Woodcock, McGrew, & Mather, 2001; 2007b; Schrank, Mather & McGrew 2014a)

- **Wechsler Individual Achievement Test** – Third Edition (Wechsler, 2009)

Emotional and behavior functioning

Comprehensive evaluations for ASD also includes social-emotional and behavior rating scales. One commonly-used general measure that includes teacher, parent, and self-report measures is the **Behavior Assessment System for Children-2** (BASC-2; Reynolds & Kamphaus, 2004), which evaluates symptoms related to depression, anxiety, AD/HD, behavior disorders, psychosis, and tic disorders, as well as clinical information specific to ASD. Similarly, the **Achenbach System of Empirically Based Assessment** (ASEBA), specifically the **Child Behavior Checklist** (CBCL; Achenbach & Rescorla, 2001), is a parent-report measure that assesses symptoms of depression, anxiety, somatic complaints, obsessive-compulsive behaviors, attention problems, social difficulties, aggressive behaviors, and atypical behaviors, with the younger version for children ages 18 months to 5 years also providing information related to ASD.

Given the comorbidity that occurs in ASD and AD/HD, it is important to also evaluate for AD/HD symptoms. A common rating scale may include the **Conners' Rating Scales** – Third Edition (Conners, 2008), which asses symptoms of AD/HD inattentive type, AD/HD hyperactive-impulsive type, oppositional defiant disorder, and conduct disorder. Other assessment measures may include computerized tests of attention, such as the:

- **Integrated Visual and Auditory Continuous Performance Test** (IVA-CPT; Sanford & Turner, 2000)

- **Test of Variables of Attention** (Leark et al., 2007).

If further evaluation is required for symptoms of AD/HD, assessment of memory and executive functioning may also be conducted. For memory, psychologists or neuropsychologists may use measures such as the:

- **Wide Range Assessment of Memory and Learning**, Second Edition (WRAML2; Sheslow & Adams, 2003)

- **Children's Memory Scale** (CMS; Cohen, 1997)

- **NEPSY-II Memory for Faces subtest** (Korkman et al., 2007)

To assess executive functioning, the **Behavior Rating Inventory of Executive Functioning** (BRIEF; Giola et al., 2000) may be used, which is another teacher and parent report measure that assesses behavioral regulation (e.g., subscales of inhibit, shift, and emotional control) and metacognition (e.g., subscales of initiate, working memory, plan/organize, organization of materials, and monitor). Other assessment measures that may be given to evaluate executive functioning include:

- **Delis-Kaplan Executive Functioning System** (D-KEFS; Delis, Kaplan, Kramer, 2001)

- **Wisconsin Card Sorting Test** (WCST, Heaton, Chelune, Talley, Kay, & Curtis, 1993)

- **Stroop Color and Word Test: Children's Version** (Golden, Freshwater, & Golden, 2004)

LANGUAGE FUNCTIONING

Given many of the social pragmatic language and communication difficulties individuals with ASD possess, it is also important to have a speech-language evaluation. A speech-language pathologist can assess language skills, social competency, phonology, dyspraxia, apraxia, articulation, hearing, voice tone and volume, oral-motor skills, and verbal fluency.

Some common single-word vocabulary tests include the:

- **Peabody Picture Vocabulary Test**, Fourth Edition (PPVT-4; Dunn & Dunn, 2007)

- **Expressive Vocabulary Test**, Second Edition (EVT2; Williams, 2007)

- **Expressive One-Word Picture Vocabulary Test** (EOWPV; Brownell, 2000)

For early language assessment, the **Clinical Evaluation of Language Fundamentals – Preschool** (CELF-P; Wiig, Semel, & Secord, 2004) assesses concepts, syntax, semantics, and morphology and is widely used. Other early language measures may include:

- **Preschool Language Scale** - Fourth Edition (Zimmerman et al., 2002)

- **Reynell Developmental Language Scales – III** (Edwards et al., 1999)

- **Tests of Early Language Development** (Hresko et al., 1999)

- **Test of Language Development** – Primary: Third Edition (Newcomer & Mammill, 1997)

More comprehensive measures, which are recommended, include the **Clinical Evaluation of Language Fundamentals** – Fourth Edition (CELF-4; Semel, Wiig, & Secord, 2003), which measures both receptive and expressive language, the **Test of Language Competence** (TLC; Wiig & Secord, 1989), and the **Comprehensive Assessment of Spoken Language** (Carrow-Woolfok, 1999).

Some examples of assessment tools for language in nonverbal individuals with ASD include:

- **Augmentative Communication Assessment Profile** (Goldman, 2002)

    O⊓ **Matching Assistive Technology and Child** (Scherer, 1997)

    O⊓ **Developmental Assessment for Individuals with Severe Disabilities**-Second Edition (DASH-2; Dykes & Erin, 1999)

    O⊓ **Communication Supports Checklist** (McCarthy et al., 1998)

SOCIAL COMMUNICATION

For pragmatic language, it is important to use some type of observational data taken during conversations with the individual that evaluates function of communication, the organization of turns and topics in conversations, flexible use of language forms in relation to specific contexts, the use of presupposition, and conversational manners (Paul & Wilson, 2009). Certain standardized tests may also be helpful, including the:

    O⊓ **Test of Pragmatic Language** (TOPL; Phelps-Terasaki & Phelps-Gunn, 1992),

    O⊓ **Children's Communication Checklist-2** (CCC-2; Bishop, 2006)

    O⊓ **The Autism Spectrum Screening Questionnaire** (ASSQ; Ehlers, Gillberg, & Wing, 1999)

    O⊓ **Pragmatic Rating Scale** (PRS; Landa et al., 1992).

Other helpful checklists or ratings include:

    O⊓ **Responsiveness/Assertiveness Rating Scale** (Girolametto, 1997)

    O⊓ **Pragmatic Protocol** (Prutting & Kirchner, 1983)

    O⊓ **Discourse Skills Checklist** (Bedrosian, 1985)

    O⊓ **Functional Communication Scales** – Revised (Kleiman, 2003)

To assess prosody (e.g., rate, volume, melody, and rhythm patterns), informal assessment is many times used, although the **Prosody-Voice Screening Profile** (PVSP; Schriberg, Kwiatkowski, & Ramussen, 1990) is sometimes used, but it requires extensive training to administer. Other social skills measures include the:

    O⊓ **Social Communication Questionnaire** (Rutter, Bailey, et al., 2003)

    O⊓ **Social Responsiveness Scale** – Second Edition (SRS-2; Constantino & Gruber, 2012)

    O⊓ **Social Language Development Test** (Bowers, Husingh, & LoGiudice, 2008)

SENSORY FUNCTIONING

One of the most frequently-used assessment measures for sensory functioning is the **Sensory Profile** (Dunn, 1999), which is a parent questionnaire. Other tools that may be used to assess sensory functioning may include the **Sensory Integration and Praxis Tests** (Ayers, 1989), as well as clinical observations.

MOTOR FUNCTIONING

There are several assessment measures that assess fine and gross motor skills. A sample of fine motor measures include:

    O⊓ **Purdue Pegboard Test** - Revised (Lafayette Instruments Company, 1999)

- 🔑 **Beery-Buktenica Developmental Test of Visual-Motor Integration** – Fifth Edition (Berry, Buktenica, & Berry, 2004)

- 🔑 **Bender Visual Motor Gestalt Test** (Bender-Gestalt II; Brannigan & Decker, 2003)

- 🔑 **Fingertip Tapping and the Imitating Hand Positions subtests from the NEPSY**-Second Edition (NEPSY-II; Korkman, Kirk, & Kemp, 2007)

- 🔑 **The Peabody Developmental Motor Scales** Second Edition (PDMS-2; Folio & Fewell, 2000)

- 🔑 **Bruininks-Oseretsky Test of Motor Proficiency**, Second Edition (BOT2; Bruininks & Bruininks, 2005)

To assess only gross motor skills, the following are used:

- 🔑 **Tests of Gross Motor Development** – Second Edition (Ulrich, 2000).

- 🔑 **Clinical Observation of Motor and Postural Skills** (COMPS), Second Edition (Wilson, Pollock, Kaplan, & Law, 1994, 2000)

- 🔑 **Movement Assessment Battery for Children**, Second Edition (Henderson, Sugden, Barnett, 2007)

Modified Checklist for Autism in Toddlers, Revised, with Follow-Up (M-CHAT-R/F)™

Diana L. Robins, Ph.D.
Deborah Fein, Ph.D. & Marianne Barton, Ph.D.

Acknowledgement: We thank the M-CHAT Study Group in Spain for developing the flow chart format used in this document.

For more information, please see www.mchatscreen.com or contact Diana Robins at DianaLRobins@gmail.com

© 2009 Diana Robins, Deborah Fein, & Marianne Barton

Permissions for Use of the M-CHAT-R/F™

The Modified Checklist for Autism in Toddlers, Revised with Follow-Up (M-CHAT-R/F; Robins, Fein, & Barton, 2009) is a 2-stage parent-report screening tool to assess risk for Autism Spectrum Disorder (ASD). The M-CHAT-R/F is available for free download for clinical, research, and educational purposes. Download of the M-CHAT-R/F and related material is authorized from www.mchatscreen.com.

The M-CHAT-R/F is a copyrighted instrument, and use of the M-CHAT-R/F must follow these guidelines:

(1) Reprints/reproductions of the M-CHAT-R must include the copyright at the bottom (2009 Robins, Fein, & Barton). No modifications can be made to items, instructions, or item order without permission from the authors.

(2) The M-CHAT-R must be used in its entirety. Evidence indicates that any subsets of items do not demonstrate adequate psychometric properties.

(3) Parties interested in reproducing the M-CHAT-R/F in print (e.g., a book or journal article) or electronically for use by others (e.g., as part of digital medical record or other software packages) must contact Diana Robins to request permission (DianaLRobins@gmail.com).

(4) If you are part of a medical practice, and you want to incorporate the first stage M-CHAT-R questions into your own practice's electronic medical record (EMR), you are welcome to do so. However, if you ever want to distribute your EMR page outside of your practice, please contact Diana Robins to request a licensing agreement.

Instructions for Use

The M-CHAT-R can be administered and scored as part of a well-child care visit, and also can be used by specialists or other professionals to assess risk for ASD. The primary goal of the M-CHAT-R is to maximize sensitivity, meaning to detect as many cases of ASD as possible. Therefore, there is a high false positive rate, meaning that not all children who score at risk will be diagnosed with ASD. To address this, we have developed the Follow-Up questions (M-CHAT-R/F). Users should be aware that even with the Follow-Up, a significant number of the children who screen positive on the M-CHAT-R will not be diagnosed with ASD; however, these children are at high risk for other developmental disorders or delays, and therefore, evaluation is warranted for any child who screens positive. The M-CHAT-R can be scored in less than two minutes. Scoring instructions can be downloaded from http://www.mchatscreen.com. Associated documents will be available for download as well.

Scoring Algorithm

For all items except 2, 5, and 12, the response "NO" indicates ASD risk; for items 2, 5, and 12, "YES" indicates ASD risk. The following algorithm maximizes psychometric properties of the M-CHAT-R:

LOW-RISK: Total Score is 0-2; if child is younger than 24 months, screen again after second birthday. No further action required unless surveillance indicates risk for ASD.

MEDIUM-RISK: Total Score is 3-7; Administer the Follow-Up (second stage of M-CHAT-R/F) to get additional information about at-risk responses. If M-CHAT-R/F score remains at 2 or higher, the child has screened positive. Action required: refer child for diagnostic evaluation and eligibility evaluation for early intervention. If score on Follow-Up is 0-1, child has screened negative. No further action required unless surveillance indicates risk for ASD. Child should be rescreened at future well-child visits.

HIGH-RISK: Total Score is 8-20; It is acceptable to bypass the Follow-Up and refer immediately for diagnostic evaluation and eligibility evaluation for early intervention.

M-CHAT-R™

Please answer these questions about your child. Keep in mind how your child usually behaves. If you have seen your child do the behavior a few times, but he or she does not usually do it, then please answer no. Please circle yes or no for every question. Thank you very much.

1. If you point at something across the room, does your child look at it?
   (**FOR EXAMPLE**, if you point at a toy or an animal, does your child look at the toy or animal?)   Yes   No

2. Have you ever wondered if your child might be deaf?   Yes   No

3. Does your child play pretend or make-believe? (**FOR EXAMPLE**, pretend to drink from an empty cup, pretend to talk on the phone or pretend to feed a doll or stuffed animal?)   Yes   No

4. Does your child like climbing on things? (**FOR EXAMPLE**, furniture, playground equipment, or stairs)   Yes   No

5. Does your child make unusual finger movements near his or her eyes?
   (**FOR EXAMPLE**, does your child wiggle his or her fingers close to his or her eyes?)   Yes   No

6. Does your child point with one finger to ask for something or to get help?
   (**FOR EXAMPLE**, pointing to a snack or toy that is out of reach)   Yes   No

7. Does your child point with one finger to show you something interesting?
   (**FOR EXAMPLE**, pointing to an airplane in the sky or a big truck in the road)   Yes   No

8. Is your child interested in other children? (**FOR EXAMPLE**, does your child watch other children, smile at them, or go to them?)   Yes   No

9. Does your child show you things by bringing them to you or holding them up for you to see – not to get help, but just to share? (**FOR EXAMPLE**, showing you a flower, a stuffed animal, or a toy truck)   Yes   No

10. Does your child respond when you call his or her name? (**FOR EXAMPLE**, does he or she look up, talk or babble, or stop what he or she is doing when you call his or her name?)   Yes   No

11. When you smile at your child, does he or she smile back at you?   Yes   No

12. Does your child get upset by everyday noises? (**FOR EXAMPLE**, does your child scream or cry to noise such as a vacuum cleaner or loud music?)   Yes   No

13. Does your child walk?   Yes   No

14. Does your child look you in the eyes when you are talking to him or her, playing with him or her, or dressing him or her?   Yes   No

15. Does your child try to copy what you do? (**FOR EXAMPLE**, wave bye—bye, clap or make a funny noise when you do)   Yes   No

16. If you turn your head to look at something, does your child look around to see what you are looking at?   Yes   No

17. Does your child try to get you to watch him or her? (**FOR EXAMPLE**, does your child look at you for praise, or say "look" or "watch me"?)   Yes   No

18. Does your child understand when you tell him or her to do something? (**FOR EXAMPLE**, if you don't point, can your child understand "put the book on the chair" or "bring me the blanket"?)   Yes   No

19. If something new happens, does your child look at your face to see how you feel about it? (**FOR EXAMPLE**, if he or she hears a strange or funny noise, or sees a new toy, will he or she look at your face?)   Yes   No

20. Does your child like movement activities? (**FOR EXAMPLE**, being swung or bounced on your knee?)   Yes   No

Chapter FIVE

Early Intervention and Treatment

The Committee on Educational Interventions for Children with Autism and National Research Council (Lord & McGee, 2001) recommends early intervention that should be intensive, individualized, and regularly evaluated where the child is educated at school, home, and in the community settings. Intervention should be a minimum of 25 hours every week, year round, in a one-on-one or small group, with parent involvement.

APPLIED BEHAVIORAL ANALYSIS

Applied Behavioral Analysis (ABA) is well documented in the autism research as an effective approach to teach new skills and behaviors, reduce maladaptive and disruptive behaviors, maintain and generalize positive behaviors, and enhance attention and motivation (Goldstein, 2002; Horner, Carr, Strain, Todd, & Reed, 2002; Lovass, 1987; Odom et al., 2003, Sallows & Graupner, 2005). We also know that early intervention is the most beneficial for children with ASD (Lovaas, 1987; Rogers & Lewis, 1989), particularly, early intensive behavioral intervention (EIBI), which applies the principles of ABA to young children. EIBI includes 25 to 40 hours per week of behavioral intervention for two or more years. Children participating in EIBI have been shown to demonstrate significant improvements in intellectual, educational, and adaptive behavior functioning (Cohen, Amerine-Dickens, & Smith, 2006; Lovaas, 1987).

There are several techniques that primarily use the theory of ABA, including Discrete Trial Training, Pivotal Response Treatment, and Verbal Behavior.

Discrete trial training

Discrete Trial Training (DTT) was created by Ole Ivar Lovaas and is the only therapy that has been approved by the United States Surgeon General's office (Department of Health, 1999). Research on DTT continues to support that it is an evidenced-based treatment (Odom, Boyd, Hall, Hume, 2010; Warren et al., 2011). DTT begins with a comprehensive assessment of skills in order to create an individualized curriculum for each child. DTT then breaks down tasks into small basic parts and uses techniques of reinforcement, prompting, shaping, and chaining to teach appropriate behaviors, all techniques that will be discussed in Chapter 6, Behavioral Strategies. Each individual task of the child's program typically consists of several brief structured teaching trials, where the child is given a prompt, then either reinforced or corrected based on their response. All data is recorded so that the child's program can be monitored, evaluated, and changed according to the child's progress. The process of "discrete trial training" and frequently-used terms is described as follows:

Discrete Trial Training

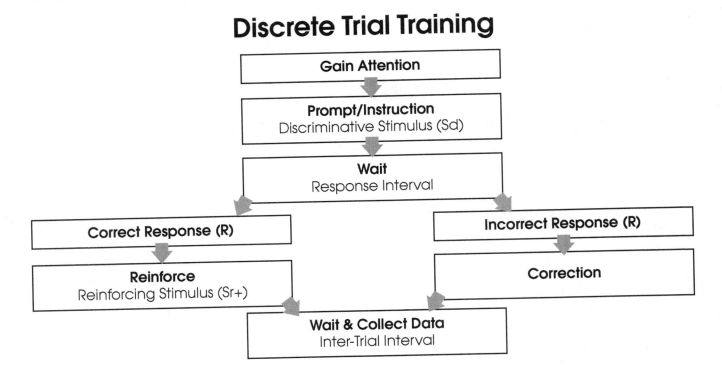

Verbal behavior

Verbal Behavior (1957) was a book written by B.F. Skinner that describes language as a set of operants, with each operant serving a specific function. A list of operants includes mands, echoics, tacts, intraverbals, and autoclitics. A mand is a request of a particular object through language. Echoic is to echo the language to obtain the desired object. Tact is to label an object. Intraverbal is to have a conversation about an object. Autoclitic is to provide a response that modifies the function of other verbal behaviors. Examples of these operants in the context of antecedents and consequences are detailed in the following pictorial. Verbal Behavior is many times used to expand the language of a child within a more comprehensive DTT behavioral program.

Case Example
SARA

Sara is a 3-year-old who is working on making requests by pointing. For each trial, she is given two objects (e.g., goldfish cracker and pretzels) in front of her. If she points independently to the preferred item (e.g., goldfish), she immediately gets the goldfish and is verbally praised for pointing to the goldfish. If she doesn't point to an item, she is physically prompted how to point to the goldfish, while being praised for pointing, and is then rewarded with the goldfish. This "trial" is presented 10 times to Sara, praising and rewarding her with the actual item each time. Prompts are faded quickly so that Sara learns to point independently.

Obsessions and Compulsions	Verbal Operant	Consequence *Example*
Motivating Operation	Mand	Directly Effective *While mom is blowing bubbles, Josh says, "more bubbles." The mom blows more bubbles.*
Verbal Behavior of Another Person (same context)	Echoic	Social *The teacher shows Mary a frog and says, "Frog." Mary says "Frog."*
Feature of the Physical Environment	Tact	Social *Ryan looks up into the sky and says, "Look mom, an airplane." His mom says, "Yes, it is."*
Verbal Behavior of Another Person (different context)	Intraverbal	Social *A teacher asks Marie, "What kind of animal barks?" Marie answers, "A dog?" "You are correct." says the teacher.*
A Person's Own Verbal Behavior	Autoclitic	Directly Effective *After playing soccer, Joe tells his mother, "I really want some water." His mother gets him a glass of water.*

Pivotal response treatment

Pivotal Response Treatment (PRT) was created by Robert Koegel and Lynn Kern Koegel (Koegel et al., 2006) and also uses the principles of ABA. PRT focuses on "pivotal" areas of development in the natural environment, including motivation, response to multiple cues, self-management, and social initiation to teach language, social communication, and academic skills and to decrease disruptive and self-stimulatory behaviors. PRT typically involves child choice, task variation, interspersing maintenance and acquisition tasks, rewarding attempts, and the use of direct natural reinforcers. Several studies have demonstrated effectiveness of PRT in case studies (Ventola, Oosting, Keifer, & Friedman, 2015), in community-based early intervention (Smith, Flanagan, Garon, & Bryson, 2015), in reducing disruptive behaviors in public school settings (Mohammadzaheri, Koegel, Rezaei, & Bakhshi, 2015), and in obtaining greater skill acquisition for parents and children in functional and adaptive communication skills (Hardan et al., 2015), although further research is still warranted on PRT to replicate these studies.

Case Example
BRIAN

Brian is a 2-year-old who is working on verbal requests. He is presented with several preferred toys in his environment (e.g., cars and a racetrack, an ice cream set, and play-doh). Brian sits next to the cars and racetrack and begins to play. The therapist sits next to him, saying 'You want to play with the cars and racetracks. It looks like we need some more cars." She then gets a clear bag of toy race cars that belongs to the racetrack. The boy sees a red car in the bag and says "red car," and the therapist then gives him the red car. The therapist continues to present a choice of preferred toys in Brian's natural environment, which he verbally requests each time and is then rewarded with the item.

DEVELOPMENTAL APPROACHES

Early Start Denver Model

A developmental approach that is also rooted in ABA is the Early Start Denver Model (ESDM). It was developed by Sally Rogers and Geraldine Dawson and combines behavioral, relational, and developmental aspects of intervention into a play-based approach that is individualized and standardized. Individualized programs are based on a comprehensive assessment of early development including cognitive skills, language, social behavior, imitation, fine and gross motor skills, self-help skills, and adaptive behavior. Skills are taught within joint activity routines that foster social learning. Studies show that ESDM is an effective intervention for toddlers with ASD for improving cognitive and adaptive functioning and reducing symptom severity (Dawson et al., 2010; Roger et al., 2012).

Floortime ®

Floortime® takes a developmental perspective, drawing on elements of ego and object relations psychology. It is based on the Developmental Individual Difference Relationship Model (DIR) created by Stanley Greenspan and Serena Wieder. The model assists the child in mastering six foundational milestones: self-regulation and interest in the world, intimacy, two-way communication, complex communication, emotional ideas and emotional thinking while helping to identify each child's unique strengths and developmental capacities. It involves following the child's lead, challenging the child to be creative and spontaneous, and then expanding the interaction to include all of the child's senses, motor skills, and different emotions. Floortime includes many elements that have been shown to be positive in the treatment of ASD, such as helping parents capitalize on incidental opportunities for instruction, teaching new skills using shaping and reinforcement, and so forth, although research is lacking (Metz et al., 2005). Only one known rigorous study supports the possible efficacy of this approach (Greenspan & Wieder, 1997), but it is not considered an evidenced-based treatment (Mercer, 2015) as further outcome research needs to be conducted.

Relationship Development Intervention

Relationship Development Intervention (RDI) is a parent-based, cognitive-developmental treatment

> ### Case Example
> ## *JACKIE*
>
> Jackie is an 18-month-old girl who is crawling around the room. She stops momentarily at a bucket of balls, at which the therapist immediately says, "You found the balls," and positions herself and Jackie to play a game of throwing the balls in a bucket. The therapist incorporates several of Jackie's goals of imitation, gross motor (throwing a ball), receptive language, expressive language, and social interaction into the activity. The therapist models throwing the ball into the bucket while saying, "Let's throw the balls into the bucket," which Jackie imitates by throwing another ball in the bucket. The therapist praises Jackie by saying, "Great throw," and then holds up a ball in front of Jackie, saying, "ball." Jackie then utters, "bbb," and is then reinforced with the ball. She throws the ball in the air and is reinforced for throwing. The interaction continues for several minutes, with the therapist introducing "ball" repeatedly and giving the ball to Jackie for any approximation of a request for the ball.

program created by Steven Gutstein. There are three training steps required for RDI: caregiver training, consultation meeting, and parent-child re-evaluation. Primary caregivers are trained to engage in joint attention, conjoint pretend play skills, social communication, and functional and adaptive behaviors with their child. The goals of the RDI program focus on the six stages of Emotion Sharing, Referencing, Coordinating Actions, Variations, Reversals and Transformations, and Co-Regulation. To date, only one non-experimental study without a control group (Gutstein, Burgess, Montfort, 2007) has been conducted demonstrating some positive effectives of RDI, thus more research is needed to assess the efficacy of this approach.

EDUCATIONAL INTERVENTIONS

TEACCH

Project TEACCH (Treatment and Education of Autistic and Communication-Handicapped Children) was first started in 1971 by Eric Schopler and Robert Reichler. TEACCH is an educational intervention in which children with ASD receive individual classroom instruction designed to accommodate learning styles characteristic of their disorder. This accommodation includes using pictures, teaching in small group settings, using a separate work station isolated from extraneous noise, and placing highly structured schedules in view of the student (Mesibov & Shea, 2009). The TEACCH method "may accelerate the development of cognitive and self-help skills" in children with ASD, and has demonstrated positive outcomes in comparison to standard special education programs for children with ASD (Ozonoff & Cathcart, 1998). Other studies have also demonstrated positive outcomes (Panerei and colleagues, 2002). TEACCH is a comprehensive, integrated program in North Carolina, yet it is difficult to replicate in other states. Many programs (outside of NC) only incorporate parts of TEACCH, which leads to inconsistent results in treatment efficacy (Metz et. al, 2005).

SCERTS

Social Communication/Emotional Regulation/Transactional Support (SCERTS) is an educational approach developed by Barry Prizant, Amy Wetherby, Emily Rubin, and Amy Laurant. SCERTS combines several models, including PRT, TEACCH, Floortime and RDI. It is a child-directed approach that focuses on social communication, emotional regulation, and transactional support. Social communication goals include the development of spontaneous, functional communication, emotional expression, and secure, trusting relationships. Goals in emotional regulation focus on the development of maintaining a regulated emotional state to cope with stress and to be available to learn and interact with others. Transactional support refers to the need to help caregivers respond to the child's needs and interests, modify and adapt the environment, and provide tools to assist learning. To date, research is lacking on this approach.

PSYCHOPHARMACOLOGY

Many children with ASD are treated with medications, although, interestingly, there is little evidence to support clear benefit for most medications (McPheeters et al., 2011). Medications for autism are most effective when given in combination with behavioral interventions such as ABA or ESDM.

To date, the Food and Drug Administration has only approved two drugs (risperidone and aripiprazole) for treating irritability in ASD. Both risperidone (Risperdal) and aripiprazole (Abilify) are antipsychotics that can be beneficial for reducing challenging and repetitive behaviors in children with ASD (McPheeters et al., 2011). Risperidone has been extensively studied (McDougle et al., 1998; McCracken et al., 2002; McDougle et al., 2005) as well as aripiprazole (Marcus et al., 2009), but both can cause adverse side effects including weight gain, sedation, and other physical symptoms (McPheeters et al., 2011).

Serotonin-reuptake Inhibitors (SRIs), such as citalopram (Celexa), escitalopram (Lexapro), and Fluoxetine (Prozac) have also been studied. Escitalopram did show some benefit for repetitive behavior, but overall, evidence demonstrates that SRIs are not effective in treating ASD (McPheeters et al., 2011). In addition, studies on stimulants (Handen et al., 2000; Quintana et al., 1995; Posey et al., 2004) may show some improvements in hyperactivity, although a review of studies shows insufficient evidence for positive effects on ASD symptoms (McPheeters et al., 2011).

REVIEWS OF EARLY INTERVENTION APPROACHES

Systematic reviews of various early intervention approaches report that models of EIBI, DTT, and ESDM all demonstrate improvements in cognitive performance, language skills, and adaptive behavior in young children with ASD (Warren et al., 2011) and studies supporting these interventions are procedurally well-documented, have been replicated, and demonstrate evidence of efficacy (Odom, Boyd, Hall, & Hume, 2010). Other models that demonstrate strengths, but need continued evaluation include PRT, DIR, TEACCH, and SCERTS (Odom, Boyd, Hall, & Hume, 2010).

Part Two

Chapter SIX

Behavioral Strategies

Behavioral strategies involve understanding all the basic components of ABA. In any behavioral program, the goal is to start with increasing desirable behaviors. This chapter will define certain behavioral terms while integrating specific strategies for clinical practice. Most of the information for this chapter was taken from an in-service training manual created with one of my colleagues (Olson & Marker, 2000) for professionals at a residential treatment facility for children with autism and other special needs.

INCREASING DESIRABLE BEHAVIORS

Reinforcement

Something serves as a reinforcement if it immediately follows a behavior and increases the frequency of that behavior in the future. If it does NOT increase the behavior, it is NOT a reinforcement for that child. It is always better to reinforce (increase) a desirable behavior than to punish (decrease) an undesirable behavior. Doing so teaches good behavior. Some literature suggests we should be giving as many as ten or more positives or reinforcers for every negative or punishment we give, which is extremely difficult. A good rule is to give at least five or six positive reinforcements to your child for every negative reinforcement you give. Just remember to make sure the reward is motivating for your child and is realistic for you to give the child.

Positive reinforcers are things that you give to a child for desirable behavior. These rewards are hierarchical, ranging from the simplest reinforcers (for young children or those with intellectual disabilities) up to more complex reinforcers (requiring a higher cognitive level and maturity).

Reinforcement Hierarchy

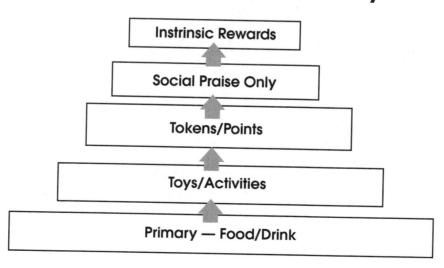

Instrinsic Rewards

Intrinsic reinforcement is the ability to enjoy self-reward and to do something because "it makes me feel good."

Social Praise Only

This level of the hierarchy involves only social reinforcement. Any child can learn to be responsive to people and can enjoy hugs and praise if it is presented consistently and carefully. Good verbal praise identifies the behavior specifically ("Good job picking up your shoes" rather than "Good boy").

Tokens/Points

At this level, we use the token economy system. Children receive tokens/points for appropriate behavior and correct responses. These tokens/points may be exchanged at a later time for a favorite reinforcer (such as food, toys, activities, etc.). We start by giving just one token/point and then immediately trade it for a reinforcer. Over time, we increase the number of tokens/points it takes to trade and the amount of work the child must do to earn each token/point.

Toys/Activities

This step involves the use of toys or special activities. This is often a powerful and under-used form of reinforcement. Many children will work hard for playing with a favorite toy, watching a favorite TV program, or going on a special outing. Variety is the key to making toys and activities effective as reinforcement!

Primary — Food/Drink

At the bottom of the hierarchy are primary reinforcers. These include food and drink, the "basics" for human life, and everyone is motivated to do what it takes to get them. When using edible reinforcers, it is important to offer only tiny portions each time so that the child does not get full. Variety is also very important. Too much of the same thing decreases its effectiveness as a reinforcer. Your child will become tired of it and will not work for it anymore. Primary reinforcers SHOULD ALWAYS be accompanied by social reinforcement (praise, attention, hugs, etc.). By pairing social reinforcement with other types of reinforcers, eventually the primary reinforcer can be dropped and the social reinforcement will be powerful enough to serve as a reinforcer by itself.

Negative reinforcers are things that are removed from the environment that increase the child's behavior. For example, if a child fakes a stomachache in order to avoid school, then avoiding school would serve as a negative reinforcer for faking a stomachache. A classic example is a child who hits another child so that the child will go away. The child leaving serves as a negative reinforcer for hitting the child.

To assist with understanding what is reinforcing to each child, it is helpful to have professionals and caregivers complete a reinforcement inventory for every child. A sample reinforcement inventory has been included at the end of this chapter for your use.

Next, we want to focus on when and how to reinforce the child or individual with ASD. Noncontingent reinforcement should be used when you first start working with a child. During a noncontingent reinforcement period, you should make you and the environment reinforcing for the child. Noncontingent reinforcement is when you create a pleasant and reinforcing environment by delivering reinforcers independent of what the child is doing.

Steps for providing contingent reinforcement

After you have become a reinforcer for your child from providing noncontingent reinforcement, you want to start providing contingent reinforcement. The child will be reinforced for a specific target behavior. Some specific principles for providing contingent reinforcement include:

1. Start reinforcing at the current behavioral level.

   At first, reinforce small steps in the right direction. Carefully observe the child to figure out what she or he can do right now. Reinforce the smallest improvements in behavior. For example, if you are working on in-seat behavior, reinforce the child for sitting for just a few seconds.

2. Reinforce immediately.

   As soon as the child performs the desired task, give the reinforcer. It is important to act quickly because the child won't understand why they are getting the reward if you act later. Be sure the child actually does some of the task; don't give a reinforcer just for saying he will try.

3. Don't wait for mastery; reinforce along the way.

   A child will learn new behaviors gradually. Recognize improvement and offer reinforcement for it. This is called "shaping" and will be discussed in-depth later.

4. When teaching new behavior, use "continuous reinforcement."

   When a new behavior is weak and unstable, reinforce it every time it happens. Be consistent! New behaviors will not be learned without regular reinforcement.

5. Use "occasional reinforcement" for stable behaviors.

   Once a behavior is mastered, call attention to it less frequently. Unpredictable reinforcement will keep the behavior going for a long time, and make it a habit.

Token economy systems

A token economy system is a set of procedures for systematically using tokens to reinforce (strengthen and/or increase) desired behavior. Goals for using token economies are to teach the value of secondary reinforcement, delay of gratification, encourage appropriate behaviors that will carry over to other settings, and to decrease inappropriate/maladaptive behaviors.

A token is any item that is given as a reward and can be exchanged at a later time for an actual reward. Tokens are generally not valuable to a child in and of themselves; children learn to value them because they know that they can trade tokens in for a toy, food, or activity they do value. Common items used for tokens are plastic markers, pennies, plastic coins, stars, or checkmarks on a tally sheet. It is most practical to use tokens that can be easily and quickly given.

Tokens are then traded for back-up reinforcers. Back-up reinforcers are the rewards that the child likes in and of themselves. They can be food, toys, or activities. Have a variety of back-up reinforcers from which the child may choose. Make sure that you choose back-up reinforcers that the child likes, rather than what you think they should like. If it is an activity, make sure that it is an appropriate one.

Rules concerning tokens:

1. A token should be something that the child can see, touch, and/or count.

2. The child must store the tokens or be able to see how many he/she has earned.

3. The child must be able to exchange the tokens for actual rewards (back-up reinforcers) as frequently as necessary to maintain the child's motivation.

4. The child should not be able to obtain a token from sources other than the parent, teacher, aide, etc.

5. The child must know that a token can be exchanged for various rewards that he/she likes, and must be able to know in advance how many tokens are needed to "purchase" particular rewards. We can tell how much they value the tokens by how they take care of them, how they respond when they are administered, and even if they try to take them from other children.

6. In some cases, tokens may be tally marks, etc., but other than this, the token should not be so large or small that the child is prevented from handling it.

When starting a token economy system, it is important to first choose a target behavior that you want to increase in your child. This target behavior should be realistic and something the child already knows how to do.

Some tips in starting a token economy system include:

1. Choose a target behavior that you want to increase in your child.

2. The child needs to know:
   • What behaviors earn tokens
   • How many tokens he/she can earn for behaviors
   • What they can trade tokens for
   • How many tokens are needed to earn different back-up reinforcers (the "cost" of the reinforcer)
   • What behaviors will cause them to lose tokens (i.e., behaviors that you want to decrease)
   • How many tokens he/she will lose for engaging in behaviors you want to decrease
   • When the tokens can be traded for back-up reinforcers ("trade time")
   • With higher-level children, it is helpful if they know how many tokens they are earning for an activity before starting.

3. If a child is able to read, it is often helpful to have a chart of what behaviors earn tokens, the "cost" of different back-up reinforcers (a reinforcement menu), and what behaviors lead to the loss of tokens. If the child is unable to read, you may use pictures of reinforcers for motivation.

4. If you are using a token system in a group setting, have set trade times in which the child counts his/her tokens to see what reinforcers (if any) they have earned.

When administering tokens, you should always pair the token with verbal praise. Physical contact is also good to give if possible (if it is reinforcing to the child). Make sure to tell the child WHY she/he earned a token (e.g., "I like the way you are sitting in your seat,", "Good job setting the table"). Tokens must be given immediately after the behavior occurs, no matter how often the behavior occurs and should be given frequently for target behaviors. The keys are to give tokens CONSISTENTLY, IMMEDIATELY, AND CONTINUOUSLY at first and as the behavior gets stronger, gradually increase the amount and difficulty of the behavior required for the same back-up reinforcer.

For lower functioning individuals, you may have to start with teaching the child to value tokens. If a child has never been on a token system before and is unable to understand an explanation of tokens, it is important to first teach him/her to value the tokens. This is done by creating an association in the child's mind between the token and the back-up reinforcer.

Tips for teaching a child to value tokens:

1. Start with just one target behavior so that the child will be aware exactly what behavior earns tokens.
2. As soon as the child engages in the target behavior, give him/her a token.
3. IMMEDIATELY have the child give you back the token
4. IMMEDIATELY give him/her a small back-up reinforcer (e.g., a raisin)
5. Continue to use immediate trade until the child learns that they are "buying" the back-up reinforcer with the token. You can then gradually increase the number of tokens the child earns before trading. For example, after a child seems to understand that by giving you the token, he/she gets a treat, let him/her earn two tokens and then trade, giving a slightly larger treat.
6. As a child advances, you can increase the amount of time between trades and/or the number of tokens needed to earn certain reinforcers.

Higher functioning individuals might use a behavior chart instead of tangible tokens. The child may earn tally marks, stars, smiley faces, or stickers on the chart. If using a behavior chart, it is important to still reinforce the child immediately after the target behavior occurs. Also, it is important to only include approximately three target behaviors on a chart as too many target behaviors can be confusing to the child and the professional.

Some schools use a daily child behavior chart where the child then gets reinforced once they are home. Remember, for something to be a reinforcer, it must immediately follow the behavior. Reinforcing the child once they are home is not a weak reinforcer. Daily child behavior charts can still be used as a communication tool between home and school, although they are difficult to use as reinforcers for the child.

If you do use a daily child behavior chart, then it is important to make it as reinforcing for the child as possible by setting them up for success. For example, the first week should just be focused on having the child enjoy the behavior chart. To do this, just put one thing on the chart that the child already knows how to do every day (e.g., says hello to teacher). Always state the target behavior in a positive way. Use words that tell the child what appropriate behavior they need to do, not the behavior you don't want them to do. For example, instead of saying "no hitting," use words like "have good hands," or "say I'm mad, please help." If the child doesn't understand "good hands" then it is ok to state first the appropriate behavior, followed by the maladaptive behavior (e.g., good hands/no hitting).

Have the parent talk with the child in the morning about the chart, telling and showing them that if they engage in the target behavior (e.g., say hello to the teacher), then they get a small reward after school. Then they should write down together some appropriate and realistic daily rewards (e.g., 15 minutes extra screen time) and weekly rewards (e.g., rent a video game) for engaging in the target behavior. Since the child can already engage in the target behavior (i.e., says hello to teacher), the child will automatically succeed. When he/she comes home from school, the child will want to show the parent the behavior chart so that they can earn their back-up reinforcer (e.g., 15 extra minutes of screen time).

Sample — Daily Child Behavior Chart - First Week

Name:	Week:						
Behavior	Mon	Tues	Wed	Thurs	Fri	Sat	Sun
Says Hello to teacher	★	★	★	★	★		
Total Smiling Faces/Stickers							

Daily Reward:	Weekly Rewards
1 Smiling Faces/Stickers =	5 Smiling Faces/Stickers =
Special Snack	Rent a Movie/Video Game
Game with Mom	Go out for ice cream
15 extra minutes of screen time	Go out to dinner

After the first week of success, add a second target behavior to the chart. Preferably this target behavior should be something the child knows how to do, but does not do it every day, maybe only half the time (e.g., good hands/no hitting). Again, we need to teach the child to value the behavior chart so we need to set them up for success. It isn't until the child is successful every day with two target behaviors, that you would add a third target behavior, as seen in the following example for Week 3.

Sample — Daily Child Behavior Chart – Third Week							
Name:	Week:						
Behavior	Mon	Tues	Wed	Thurs	Fri	Sat	Sun
Says Hello to teacher	★		★	★	★		
Good Hands (No hitting)	★	★	★	★		★	★
Plays a game with friend during free time		★	★	★	★	★	★
Total Smiling Faces/Stickers	2	2	3	3	2	2	2

Daily Reward:	Weekly Reward:
2-3 Smiling Faces/Stickers =	14-21 Smiling Faces/Stickers =
Special Snack	Rent a Movie/Video Game
Game with Mom	Go out for ice cream
15 extra minutes of screen time	Go out to dinner

Worksheet

Daily Child Behavior Chart

Name: _____

Week: _____

Behavior	Mon	Tues	Wed	Thurs	Fri	Sat	Sun

Total Smiling Faces/Stickers

Daily Reward:

Weekly Reward:

Prompts

The next behavioral term used frequently is prompt or prompting. Prompts are cues given by others in order to obtain the desired response. Prompts direct the learner's attention to the task at hand and its requirements. The purpose of a prompt is to give staff an opportunity to reinforce the desired behavior when it occurs. There are several types of prompts. Depending upon your goal, you may want to use the least restrictive prompt (the one that offers the least amount of direction), which encourages as much independent behavior as possible and gives your child plenty of opportunity to show you what he/she can do by him/herself. Below is a hierarchy visual of prompts of least restrictive (independent) to most restrictive (physical prompts):

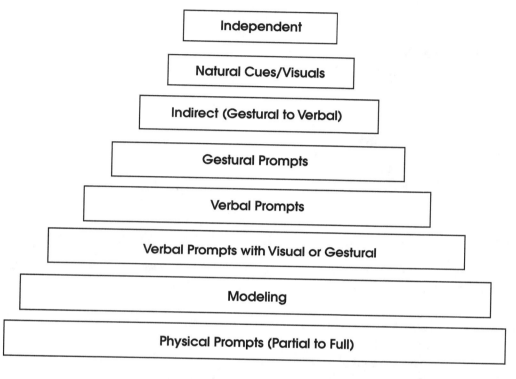

Prompts are meant to be positive teaching tools, yet many times I've observed prompts beings used as a punishment. The following case example is a negative example of using prompting.

Case Example — Negative Prompt

LILY

Lily is an 8-year-old, nonverbal child, with level three ASD. One of her IEP goals is the integration of a fine motor and academic task, which requires her to draw a square (which she was able to do yesterday with some physical prompts). She is in a self-contained classroom with six other children; some are higher functioning than her. She was given a verbal prompt, "Lily, please draw the square." After the verbal prompt, Lily sits at her desk and begins to rock. Since the teacher and assistant are actively involved in teaching others in the class, Lily rocks for five minutes. After five minutes, she is given a verbal prompt, "Lily, draw the square," with a gestural prompt (e.g., teacher points to sample square, her pencil and her paper). Lily continues to rock for several minutes. The teacher then takes Lily's hand, puts the pencil in her hand, and physically guides Lily to draw the entire square.

The use of prompts in this example failed. Based on this example, Lily did not learn anything. It became a goal of compliance instead of a fine motor/academic task. If I were Lily, I would think I was being punished instead of being taught. Yet, this is a common occurrence I have observed with professionals. Many times, we are given specific goals for our children that may be too complex and we are not given enough time to teach the goal properly. Because of this, many times we are just teaching our children compliance in the classroom instead of educating them. Imagine this same scenario, but with correct and positive prompting:

Case Example — Positive Prompt

LILY

Lily was given the follwoing visual prompt:

 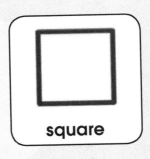

Made with Boardmaker® and the Picture Communication Symbols © 1981-2010
Mayer-Johnson LLC - 2100 Wharton St. Suite 400. Pittsburgh, PA 15203 U.S.A. Phone (800)588-4548. www.mayer-johnson.com

After this prompt, Lily sits at her desk and begins to rock. The teacher immediately comes over to Lily and starts reinforcing Lily at her current behavioral level. Her teacher points to Lily's pencil and praises Lily, "Nice looking at your pencil." The teacher then picks up Lily's pencil to show her visually to pick up the pencil. Lily still doesn't respond. The teacher gently guides Lily's hand to the pencil and praises her for touching the pencil, "Nice, touching the pencil." Lily picks up the pencil correctly, for which she is praised, "Lily, great job picking up the pencil." The teacher then models drawing one straight line and then verbally prompts Lily, "Your turn to draw the line." As Lily attempts to draw the straight line, her teacher praises her, "Nice job drawing, Lily." The teacher models the next line to complete the square at which Lily then tries to independently draw herself. Her teacher again praises each step, "Nice line, Lily." The teacher continues to visually model each line of the square and reinforcing Lily for each step completed.

Lily independently began to complete this task based on the teacher's positive prompts and praise. Also, each of the prompts contained a visual cue, which is extremely important when prompting an individual with ASD.

If your goal is to teach a new behavior or teach compliance, then you would likely start with a more restrictive prompt, such as physical prompts. When using more restrictive prompts, it is very important to fade out your prompts as quickly as possible. Fading is the behavioral term for the gradual elimination of prompts so that the learner is responding to the minimal cues that exist in the natural environment. Fading is used when a new behavior has been established and the child no longer needs as much direction. As soon as the behavior occurs without hesitation at your prompt, it's time to start fading the prompt. The purpose of fading is to increase the child's independent performance of the behavior so that the child does not rely on prompts to perform the behavior.

We may start with a physical prompt (with a verbal prompt), move to a gestural prompt (with a verbal prompt), then to a verbal prompt alone, and eventually to no prompt. Some children may also become too dependent on verbal prompts, which may require fading to a gestural prompt alone. Another way to fade a prompt is to decrease the intensity of a level of prompt. That is, if the child requires a physical prompt, you can reduce the amount of pressure of your touch. If the child requires gestural prompts, you can reduce the size of your gesture. If the child requires a verbal prompt, you can speak more softly. Reducing the intensity is usually necessary when a child has become dependent on one type of prompt and is unable to move to the less intrusive type of prompt. The key to preventing prompt dependence is to fade prompts quickly, as soon as you see the child understands. At our center, we use visuals as one of the least restrictive prompts. If the primary language is visual for individuals with ASD, then it makes sense that all our prompts should include a visual.

Shaping

The next behavioral teaching term is shaping. Shaping is a procedure used to teach a single basic behavior. To shape a response, we start with a behavior a child can already perform and reinforce each step in the right direction.

Steps in shaping

1. Observe the child to determine exactly what abilities the child displays in connection with the target behavior. We break down the behavior into little parts to see what the child CAN do.
2. Arrange the setting for the maximum likelihood that the behavior will occur. If the behavior involves other people, or if particular environmental cues are necessary, arrange to have them present during shaping.
3. Define the first approximation/step in the right direction that you will reinforce.
4. Reinforce steps in the right direction toward the target response. Use the most powerful reinforcers you can. Reward these in-between steps with lots of praise, a hug, or whatever is reinforcing for your child.
5. Use verbal, gestural, or physical prompts (only what's necessary) at all stages of the process.

Chaining

Chaining is used to teach a more complex series of behaviors. Chaining teaches a sequence of related behaviors, each of which provides the cue for the next, and the last of which produces a completed task.

The goal of chaining is to tie together already existing behaviors (which may have been shaped previously) so the child can do the sequence independently – without any verbal prompting for "what comes next." Behaviors we chain include eating breakfast, setting the table, getting dressed or undressed, and going to the bathroom. Forward chaining is when you start by reinforcing after the child does the first behavior in the sequence. Backward chaining is when you reinforce after the last step in the sequence and then you fade your prompts backward.

Steps in chaining

1. Divide the desired behavior into steps. The size of the steps will be determined by the abilities of the child.
2. Determine which steps already exist and which ones will need to be individually shaped.
3. Shape the behaviors which need to be learned, and then the chaining begins. Chaining can be started from the first step and move toward the last step OR it can start from the last step and move forward toward the first step. Whichever you choose, use that method consistently.

Case Example
BRETT

Brett is a 12-year-old nonverbal male with level three ASD whose parents brought him into the office to work on toilet training. Despite having a more severe intellectual disability, Brett was able to indicate when he was wet and wanted his diaper changed by touching his pants. Many times he would go to a corner of the house when he had to go to the bathroom. This indicated that he had the muscle control required to teach toilet training. I started to break down each step of going to the bathroom with his parents to find out if he could perform each step. "Can he walk into the bathroom?" "Yes." "Can he pull down his pants?" "Yes, if they are elastic." "Can he sit on the toilet?" The parents said, "Well. . .we have to force him." That revealed that we still needed to "shape" the behavior of sitting on the toilet. Brett's favorite thing was watching "Thomas the Tank Engine", so his parents put a VHS player and small TV in the bathroom so that we had an immediate reinforcer for Brett. To "shape" sitting on the toilet, we had to break that behavior down into even smaller parts. Brett sits on a regular chair without prompting, but not a toilet. So first, we had him fully clothed and asked him to walk into the bathroom. We then played his video. Then we asked him to sit on the toilet fully clothed while he watched his video, which Brett did. Next time, we asked Brett to walk in the bathroom, pull down his pants (not his underwear) and sit on the toilet, which he did and he watched his video. Then, we asked Brett to walk in the bathroom, pull down his pants and underwear and sit on the toilet, which he refused to do. This demonstrated that there was something about the toilet seat itself and his bare bottom that was interfering with him sitting on the toilet (i.e., maybe the cold porcelain toilet seat?). The parents got a squishy toilet seat and we started the process again. He walked into the bathroom, pulled down his pants and underwear, and then touched the toilet seat with his hands. We played the video. Next, we asked him to sit on the toilet seat, which he did and actually went to the bathroom! Imagine his parents' excitement! He was so proud of himself (and probably proud of us for figuring out that he didn't like the toilet seat!). This is a great example of shaping sitting on the toilet and then chaining together all the behaviors for going to the bathroom.

DECREASING BEHAVIORS

We started this chapter with increasing desirable behaviors, now it is time to talk about decreasing maladaptive behaviors. Remember, it's always better to increase desirable behaviors first. When we talk about the term "punishment," by definition, something serves as punishment if it immediately follows a behavior and decreases the frequency of that behavior in the future.

Examples of punishment include ignoring undesirable behavior, time out, response cost, and physical restraint. You should only use a punisher when a reinforcement strategy has failed or if you need immediate control over a dangerous behavior, such as one where someone may be injured. Remember, your first approach is to use positive reinforcers and teaching strategies (prompting, shaping, fading, chaining). A good strategy for avoiding undesirable behaviors is to keep your child busy with toys and tasks.

We can decrease unwanted behaviors through a variety of methods. The following list ranges from least to most intrusive:

1. Extinction/Ignoring

2. Differential reinforcement of other (DRO)

3. Response cost

4. Time Out

5. Physical restraint

You should use the least intrusive punisher whenever appropriate so that the child has the opportunity to have the most independent control over his or her actions.

Although punishment can suppress behavior when used correctly, it has its disadvantages. It is not the best way to change behavior because the child may try to avoid future punishment by doing less in general (the fewer "things" you do, the less likely you are to get punished). Repeated punishment leads to withdrawal in humans and animals. This can take the form of social withdrawal, depression, or lack of motivation. One way to avoid this is to make sure the child knows what behavior leads to being punished, so only that specific behavior will decrease. Punishment may also produce emotional behavior. The child may become nervous or upset prior to being punished. Also, the child may become aggressive toward the parent, staff, or children. Furthermore, negative modeling may occur. This means there is the risk of teaching the child how to react when others are not doing what they want. You serve as a role model, thus they may imitate your behavior. Lastly, the child may attempt to escape or avoid the punishment by avoiding the punisher, even when the child is not being punished. By giving at least five or six reinforcers for every one punishment, the side effects of punishment are less likely to occur.

Extinction

Extinction, or ignoring, is a behavior term that involves removing social reinforcement from a behavior that previously got lots of attention. Extinction is used when you have control over the reinforcement. When ignoring a behavior, avoid eye contact, continue with whatever you were doing before the behavior began, and maintain a calm and even tone of voice. Do not talk about the behavior or change your facial expression. You may even try turning your back to the child. Always ignore behaviors that are attempts to get your attention or to get a reaction. Extinction does not work well for self-stimulating behaviors because the reinforcement occurs within the child.

Expectations with extinction

1. Extinction only works when paired with reinforcement for the appropriate behavior.
2. Consistently withholding reinforcement results in a gradual decrease in the target behavior.
3. When you first start using extinction, there will be a brief period when the target behavior will increase. This increase is called an extinction burst. An extinction burst is an indication that the extinction is working!
4. Extinction may trigger aggression.
5. Behavior that is firmly established is more resistant to extinction (e.g., behavior that has been intermittently reinforced in the past).
6. Behavior that has been extinguished may return later, especially if you did not reinforce the competing behavior sufficiently. Be careful not to reinforce a behavior that had previously been extinguished by reacting either verbally or with your facial expression!
7. Consistency is the key!

Differential reinforcement of other (DRO)

Differential reinforcement is a procedure that combines extinction and reinforcement to change the frequency of a behavior. The undesirable behavior is ignored. An alternate behavior is reinforced. There are two types of DRO: (1) DRO of incompatible behaviors and (2) DRO of other people.

DRO of incompatible behaviors is when you reinforce an adaptive alternative behavior while ignoring the maladaptive behavior. This results in an increase of the good behavior while simultaneously preventing the misbehavior from occurring. To use DRO of other people, the desired behavior is reinforced in other people and no attention is given to the child who is engaging in the maladaptive behavior.

Response cost

Response cost is a form of punishment in which previously earned reinforcers are taken away when an undesirable behavior occurs. Response cost only works if you have been consistently reinforcing the child for appropriate behaviors up to that point.

Tips for using response cost

1. Always use reinforcement for appropriate behaviors if you are going to use response cost.

2. You must make sure that the child has a previously given reinforcer.

3. Determine and teach the child what reinforcer they will lose for which specific behavior before the behavior occurs and response cost is used.

4. Give the child 2 pieces of information: (1) why he/she lost the reinforcer and (2) how to earn the reinforcer again.

5. Take away the reinforcer immediately after the unwanted behavior occurs.

6. Be sure the child can earn back the lost reinforcer fairly quickly (this will depend on the level of the child).

7. Make sure fines are realistic. Only take one reinforcer at a time.

8. Response cost must be used consistently with all individuals working with the child. If it is not used consistently, the behavior may worsen.

Case Example
CONNIE

Connie is an 8-year-old girl with level two ASD who has a history of screaming to get others' attention. She is being taught to raise her hand instead of scream. When she screams, the teacher ignores her, but when she raises her hand, she praises her by saying, "Connie, thanks for raising you hand." When DRO of incompatible behaviors was first used, Connie's behavior worsened as she began to scream louder for attention and then even began to hit staff in the stomach. If the staff would have given her attention when she screamed louder or when she hit, then they would have reinforced screaming louder or hitting. Instead, they ignored those behaviors, praised her when she was quiet, and shaped raising her hand and giving her lots of reinforcement and attention for doing so. Now that she knows how to raise her hand, the teacher uses DRO of other people. When Connie screams, the teacher ignores the scream and then praises and gives lots of attention to those in the class who are raising their hand. When Connie visually sees that others are getting attention for raising their hands, she then stops screaming and raises her hand. The teacher immediately praises Connie and gives her attention for raising her hand.

Case Example
TOM AND CARTER

Tom and Carter are playing with Legos, but they continue to fight over a specific Lego toy. The therapist approaches the two boys and says that they need to share. If they continue to fight over the toy, then she will take away the Legos. After a couple minutes, the boys fight again for the specific part. The therapist comes back and says, "I'm sorry, you lost the Legos because you couldn't share. You can earn the Legos back after you two can show me you can share after playing basketball." She then directs them over to the basketball game. After they play basketball for 5 minutes and demonstrate they can share, the therapist praises them for sharing and tells them they can play Legos again.

Time out

Time Out is a method used to decrease inappropriate behavior. It involves removing the child from a reinforcing situation after an undesirable behavior has occurred. There are several options for Time Out, which range from least to most restrictive:

- Non-Exclusionary (e.g., child remains in setting, but all reinforcing activities have been temporarily removed)

- Exclusionary (e.g., child is moved to another part of the setting and all reinforcing activities have been removed)

- Isolation/Seclusion (e.g., child is moved to a separate Time Out room)

The least restrictive option should always be used first. Withholding reinforcement during Time Out may be more difficult than it sounds. You must withhold all social reinforcement such as eye contact, smiles, physical contact, or any other form of interaction.

Tips for using time out

1. Always use reinforcement for desirable behavior outside of Time Out.

2. Time Out areas should be free of attractive and entertaining activities (e.g., TV, toys, other people).

3. Time Out should be short. Two to five minutes can sometimes be enough. A good rule of thumb is a minute for every year of their age. It is not the amount of time that the child is in Time Out that makes it effective. It's the being put in Time Out that modifies the behavior. The child will only understand the benefit of being calm if he/she comes out of Time Out when they are calm. If left too long, the child does not understand "what it takes" to get out. Don't be concerned about having to take the child back to Time Out too quickly. It will give the child additional opportunities to learn that "calm" behavior gets them out.

4. Monitor the child in Time Out, but do not let him/her catch you watching.

5. You decide when a child is ready to leave Time Out. The child must be calm and quiet before leaving Time Out.

6. Reinforce other children (if available) for their good behavior. The child in Time Out will hear how much fun/reinforcement the other children are having.

7. Redirect the child quickly after leaving Time Out. Do not discuss the maladaptive behavior that led to going to Time Out at this time. Use a different teachable moment to talk about the maladaptive behavior. It's more important to redirect the child back to a task after Time Out.

8. Be aware that some children may use Time Out to avoid doing other tasks (e.g., school work, cleaning, etc.). Be sure the child completes the other tasks he or she missed during Time Out.

Physical restraint

Physical restraint is defined as any manual method, physical or mechanical, that immobilizes an individual. There are many types of restraints, such as positional (prone, supine, physical), mechanical (straps, helmets, other devices), and chemical (medication). Although certain restraints, if used properly, can help prevent injury, they can also be extremely dangerous. In most states, restraints can be used if the individual is an imminent danger of serious harm to self or others. In 2009, the United States Government Accountability Office conducted a study on seclusion and restraints in public and private schools and treatment centers. They reported a completed list of state laws pertaining to restraints in their report, which should be reviewed by anyone considering the use of restraints in their practice. There are several agencies that teach physical restraint to those who feel it necessary. The strategies taught by agencies to staff vary, with some using pain-compliance techniques used in marital arts, or by police, and others using pain-free techniques. I have observed restraints used both positively and negatively. Given the ethical dilemmas that can arise with the use of restraints, we choose not to use physical restraints at our agencies.

ABC ANALYSIS

An ABC Analysis is a process for gathering information about the environmental stimuli that are controlling the behavior. It includes antecedents, behavior, and consequences.

Antecedents (A)

Antecedents are things or situations which happen before the target behavior. Examples of antecedents are asking a question, time of day, loud noise, a particular toy, etc. Certain behavior may regularly follow each of these antecedents.

The first step in an ABC analysis is the antecedent analysis. By paying attention before a behavior happens, you can identify situations that may affect the likelihood of the behavior happening again. You can work to control these conditions and improve your child's behavior.

There are several types of antecedents (also environmental stimuli):

1. *Child cues:* Come before a behavior. Observing the child's characteristics or expressions before he engages in the maladaptive behavior can be extremely helpful.

2. *Prompts* that have been reinforced in the past. Are there specific phrases that lead to a maladaptive behavior?

3. *Situations:* Increase the likelihood of a behavior occurring. Many times, unstructured situations are antecedents (e.g., lining up in a line, transitions, etc.).

4. *People*: Problem behavior may occur with some people and not others. If that is the case for your child, you need to determine what's different about each person. It could be something as simple as the person's deodorant that is upsetting the child.

5. *Time of Day*: Some behaviors occur more frequently during a specific time of day. This information is useful in analyzing the particular circumstances during problematic and non-problematic periods. You may need to reschedule an activity or research the side effects of the child's medication.

6. *Activity*: Sometimes a specific activity can be related to behaviors. This information may suggest the demands and outcomes of that activity that the person may not like.

7. *Physical Setting:* The surrounding may affect behavior. Some children need quiet study areas; others need music to calm them.

Behavior (B)

This is the target behavior we are studying. It is very important to operationally define the behavior. Others will easily recognize the behavior if the behavior is described in detail. Information such as the intensity, frequency, and duration of the behavior is important to include the definition.

Consequences (C)

Consequences are things or situations which immediately follow a particular behavior. They serve two purposes: (1) to increase the behavior or (2) to decrease the behavior that just happened.

Functional Analysis

After the antecedent analysis, we then perform a functional analysis. According to behaviorism, all behavior services one of two functions (1) to obtain something desirable or (2) to avoid something undesirable. From a behavioral point of view, all behavior serves some function. By identifying the variables that maintain a behavior, we can also identify more adaptive ways of obtaining the same function.

Classification of Obtaining

In analyzing the function of obtaining something desirable, you can classify the individual's behavior into one of three categories: (1) an attempt to obtain communication, (2) an activity, or (3) an internal stimulation using examples below.

1. Obtain communication/attention

   If you believe that a child's behavior serves to obtain communication/attention, then the child will perform this behavior more often if he/she gets attention. We would want to teach the child a more adaptive behavior for obtaining communication/attention.

2. Obtain activity/task/item

   A child's behavior may be to obtain an activity, task, or item (e.g., drink, food). They may be bored and need something to do. If their behavior attempt is inappropriate, then we would want to teach them a more appropriate way to gain the activity.

3. Obtain internal stimulation

   A child may engage in a behavior in order to stimulate him/herself internally. In some cases, self-injurious behavior occurs for self-stimulation. The child may also be bored or may enjoy the sensory stimulation. As a result, you may try to teach the child another way of stimulating him/herself more appropriately.

Classification of Avoiding

If the individual performs a behavior to avoid something, it may be to avoid the same three categories: (1) communication, (2) activity, or (3) internal stimulation. Once we know what they are trying to avoid, we can teach them a more appropriate way to avoid that communication, activity, or internal stimulation.

1. Avoid communication/attention

   Sometimes maladaptive behavior may occur when a child wants to be left alone. As an adaptive behavior, you may want to teach the child a more appropriate way of asking for a break.

2. Avoid activity/task/item

   Escape of tasks and demands is very common. A child may perform a maladaptive behavior to get out of doing a task. Make sure to monitor the difficulty of tasks.

3. Avoid internal stimulation

   Some children have difficulty with internal stimulation. They may be overly sensitive or may not like a particular type of stimulation. If the child is rocking and then leaving the room when the bell is ringing, you would then want to teach the child how to avoid the sound of the bell ringing more appropriately (e.g., request to leave the room before the bell rings, request sound cancellation head phones right before the bell rings).

We can learn to watch for cues the child gives, prompt the child consistently, and create situations where good behavior is likely to happen. Success comes partly from the professionals making an environment which prevents inappropriate behaviors from occurring by paying attention before and after a behavior.

ABC Analysis

Directions: Read the following case examples and then write the antecedent, behavior, and consequences for each case. Next, identify the function of the behavior and then write a more appropriate behavior to teach. Correct answers are provided on the next page.

> **A= Stands for Antecedent** or what happens before the behavior. Antecedents can be a person, place, time, command, object, smell, noise, etc.
>
> **B= Stands for Behavior.** Behaviors are functional, meaning they serve a purpose. Behaviors most often are used to obtain or avoid something. Behaviors should be described in detail.
>
> **C= Stands for Consequences** or what happens immediately following the behavior. Consequences either reinforce or punish the behavior.

Case Example #1: Joe is playing a video game when his mother tells him to brush his teeth. Joe continues to play the video game and doesn't respond to his mother. Five minutes later, his mother asks Joe to brush his teeth again.

A = Antecedent	B = Behavior	C = Consequences

Function: To obtain and/or to avoid communication/attention, activity/task/item, or internal stimulation.

Appropriate Behavior to Teach:

Case Example #2: While playing with kids at recess, Angela calls Bob a mean name. Bob pushes Angela and knocks her to the ground. The other kids run away.

A = Antecedent	B = Behavior	C = Consequences

Function: To obtain and/or to avoid communication/attention, activity/task/item, or internal stimulation.

Appropriate Behavior to Teach:

Case Example #3: During class, several students are talking in structured small groups while Ally rocks back and forth. Ally runs out of the classroom.

A = Antecedent	B = Behavior	C = Consequences

Function: To obtain and/or to avoid communication/attention, activity/task/item, or internal stimulation.

Appropriate Behavior to Teach:

From Olson & Marker (2000). In-service Training Manual – Pine Grove School.

ABC Analysis

Directions: Read the following case examples and then write the antecedent, behavior, and consequences for each case. Next, identify the function of the behavior and then write a more appropriate behavior to teach.

> **A= Stands for Antecedent** or what happens before the behavior. Antecedents can be a person, place, time, command, object, smell, noice, etc.
>
> **B= Stands for Behavior.** Behaviors are functional, meaning they serve a purpose. Behaviors most often are used to obtain or avoid something. Behaviors should be described in detail.
>
> **C= Stands for Consequences** or what happens immediately following the behavior. Consequences either reinforce or punish the behavior.

Case Example #1: Joe is playing a video game when his mother tells him to brush his teeth. Joe continues to play the video game and doesn't respond to his mother. Five minutes later, his mother asks Joe to brush his teeth again.

A = Antecedent	B = Behavior	C = Consequences
Mother tells Joe to brush his teeth	Joe continues to play video game	Joe continues to play video game, five minutes later, mother asks again.

Function: To obtain and/or to avoid communication/attention, activity/task/item, or internal stimulation. **Obtain video game, avoid brushing teeth**

Appropriate Behavior to Teach: **When Joe can play video game, visual schedule for video game and tooth brushing, prime for how much time he has to play video games before brushing teeth**

Case Example #2: While playing with kids at recess, Angela calls Bob a mean name. Bob pushes Angela and knocks her to the ground. The other kids run away.

A = Antecedent	B = Behavior	C = Consequences
Angela calls Bob a mean name	Bob pushes Angela	Kids run away

Function: To obtain and/or to avoid communication/attention, activity/task/item, or internal stimulation. **Obtains/ommunicates anger, avoid kids**

Appropriate Behavior to Teach: **Before getting to recess, teach how to communicate feelings and ask for help. Reinforce positive interactions while at recess. Teach Bob where to go or what to do when he needs to avoid other kids at recess**

Case Example #3: During class, several students are talking in structured small groups while Ally rocks back and forth. Ally runs out of the classroom.

A = Antecedent	B = Behavior	C = Consequences
Group Activity	Ally rocks back and forth	Ally runs out of the classroom

Function: To obtain and/or to avoid communication/attention, activity/task/item, or internal stimulation. **Obtain internal stimulation/calming mechanism, avoid group activity**

Appropriate Behavior to Teach: **Before starting group activity, teach Ally how to request seat cushion if rocking becomes distracting. If ally needs a break, teach Ally how to ask for a break.**

From Olson & Marker (2000). In-service Training Manual – Pine Grove School.

Worksheet
Reinforcement Inventory

Child_____ Date_____

Person Completing Form_____

A child's reinforcers change frequently. It is important to keep track of each child's reinforcers and re-evaluate them on a weekly basis.

Instructions: Record any possible reinforcers and then rate on a scale from **doesn't like** to **likes a lot**.

Primary – Food/Drink	Doesn't Like	Neutral	Likes	Likes a lot
Types of Chips/Snacks (e.g., cheese curls, Doritos, goldfish)				
Types of Cookies (e.g., chocolate chip, Oreos, animal crackers)				
Types of Cereals (e.g., Cheerios, Fruit Loops, Kix)				
Types of Candy (e.g., Skittles, M&Ms, Gummy Bears)				
Types of Drinks (e.g., fruit punch, lemonade, soda pop)				

Toys/Activities	Does not Like	Neutral	Likes	Likes a lot
TV Shows and Movies (e.g., Sponge Bob, Avengers, Thomas the Tank Engine)				
Video Games (e.g., Minecraft, Wii games, Playstation games)				
Music (e.g., classical, plays piano, pop music)				
Specific Toys (e.g., Sesame Street pop-up, bubble gun, trucks)				
Specific Indoor Activities (e.g., crafts, board games, drawing)				
Specific Outdoor Activities (e.g., biking, hiking, go to mall)				

Toys/Activities	Does not Like	Neutral	Likes	Likes a lot
Sensory Activities (e.g., smells, colors, certain noises, rocking, touch)				
Tokens (e.g., smiley faces, points, money, charts)				
Social Praise				
By Whom? (e.g., mom, dad, brother, behavior tech)				
Touch (e.g., hugs, pat on back, high five)				
Voice Tone and Volume (e.g., high, low, certain phrases)				
Other Reinforcers?				

Chapter SEVEN

Social Communication Strategies

VISUAL COMMUNICATION STRATEGIES

Picture Exchange Communication System (PECS)

PECS is a simple process in which an individual with ASD exchanges a picture of the desired item for the actual item. The technique of PECS teaches functional communication and is many times used within an ABA program. Many studies have shown PECS to be effective with individuals with autism and other neurodevelopmental disorders (Hourcade, Pilotte, West, & Parette, 2004).

There are several types of PECS, including black and white, colored, and real pictures, as well as PECS apps on smart phones and tablets. Given that most individuals with ASD typically attend to one aspect of a picture at a time, it is best to use pictures with minimal details. Examples of these images are below:

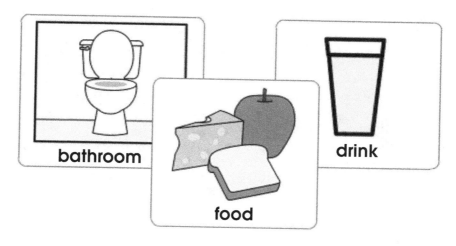

Made with Boardmaker® and the Picture Communication Symbols © 1981-2010 Mayer-Johson LLC - 2100 Wharton St. Suite 400. Pittsburgh, PA 15203 U.S.A. Phone (800)588-4548. www.mayer-johson.com

PECS should be used with both low and high functioning individuals with ASD. Given that the primary language for individuals with ASD is visual, caregivers and professionals should be using PECS more than verbal communication. If the goal for the individual with ASD is to understand verbal communication, then it is best to pair verbal communication with the PECS for the first prompt or instruction. After that, it is best to use nonverbal communication to redirect the individual with ASD back to the PECS.

For lower functioning individuals with ASD, PECS may be as simple as having the most common communication cards (e.g., bathroom, food, drink, break, help, play, etc.) on a key ring or in a binder for the individual with ASD to carry around. They can then point, exchange, or match the card to another card to communicate. For higher functioning individuals with ASD, PECS is extremely helpful in creating visual schedules or in teaching a new skill.

Case Example
LOGAN

Logan is a nine-year-old boy diagnosed with level two ASD. In the mornings, he typically takes a long time to get ready before he gets on the bus. Many mornings, he would just walk downstairs in his pajamas and begin playing games on his tablet. His parents found it extremely difficult to transition him to a different schedule. Most mornings, his parents would end up yelling and screaming at Logan to get off of the tablet. This would be followed by constantly reminding him to get dressed, brush his teeth, eat breakfast, and so forth. In Logan's mind, part of his morning routine was to go downstairs and play video games on his tablet so he did not recognize that he was doing anything wrong. To help Logan process the situation better, his parents needed to use more visual and less verbal communication. In response, Logan and his parents created a visual PECS schedule for the morning. Logan assisted in the creation of the PECS schedule and was able to identify what tasks were required before he got on the bus. The PECS schedule was placed next to Logan's bed so that in the morning, he could be reminded of what tasks were required of him before getting on the bus. His parents paired this with reinforcing Logan with additional video game time on his tablet after school. If Logan appeared off task, his parents would just point to the next step on the PECS schedule. They found that it was most useful to use nonverbal communication instead of verbal communication to help Logan follow directions.

Made with Boardmaker® and the Picture Communication Symbols © 1981-2010 Mayer-Johson LLC - 2100 Wharton St. Suite 400. Pittsburgh, PA 15203 U.S.A. Phone (800)588-4548. www.mayer-johson.com

VERBAL COMMUNICATION STRATEGIES

Despite visual information being the primary language for individuals with ASD, they do live in a verbal society. When teaching any new skill, it is extremely important to use visual and verbal teaching methods with an individual with ASD. If the goal for that individual is to process and understand auditory information, then the first skill to teach is gaining attention.

Eliminate distractions

In order to gain attention from an individual with ASD, it is important to first reduce distraction. This is much harder than you would think. Imagine being distracted by someone's perfume, or rain on the window, or your pants being too tight. We may not know what is distracting to many of the individuals with whom we work. Despite this, you have control over your environment and can eliminate distracting lights (use natural light), distracting colors (use one calming color and not a lot of stimulating colors), use fragrance free deodorant, hairspray, and shampoos, make sure the carpet is not distracting, and teach in an area that handles sound well (e.g., think of the difference of the sounds between a large supermarket, a small room, or being outside).

Assess your nonverbal communication

While teaching an individual with ASD, you want to consider that prompts you may usually use with typical individuals may be distracting to an individual with ASD. Think about your own nonverbal communication that may be distracting. For example, assess your own body language, hand gestures, and facial expressions. Many times, certain individuals may be more expressive with their nonverbal body language. Stereotypically, most women are much more expressive when it comes to their nonverbal communication compared to men. In addition, monitor your verbal communication. Assess your voice tone, intonation, and volume. Also, assess the number of words you are using. Stereotypically, women change their voice tone more often, use various intonations, and are much louder when they communicate verbally compared to men. Women also tend to multi-task more than men, whereas men typically focus on one piece of information at a time and talk less frequently than women. Interestingly, many individuals with ASD have verbalized that it is much easier to understand males than females during verbal conversations. Most importantly, use visuals when talking with individuals with ASD. A good habit is to write down what you are saying while you are talking. It is easy to write things down on a white board or a on a piece of paper. Typically, if you are writing down what you are saying, the rate at which you talk will slow down and you will be providing a visual for the individual with ASD.

Focus on proximity

Next, you want to focus on proximity. When teaching an individual with ASD, you want to be at a distance that is one arm's length away and at a 90° angle. If you're teaching an individual from across a table, they may be distracted by sound on either side of them. If you are at a 90° angle, you will be monopolizing the ear on one side of their head, so that they will only be distracted by extraneous noise on the other side.

It is also important to only be one arm's length away when you need the individual's attention. If the child is working independently, give them space. Many times I have seen aides and paraprofessionals sitting too close to the individual, which can be very distracting to that individual while they are working.

Identify the goal and prompt

When teaching anyone with ASD, it is important to have a clear understanding of what the goal is for that individual. If your goal is to teach a new skill, then it may be in that individuals' best interest for you to use the most restrictive prompt. If, however, the individual already knows the specific skill, then your goal may be for the individual to process the contextual information around them. In that case, it would be best to use the least restrictive prompt. After you have provided an appropriate prompt, then you need to allow time for processing.

Allow time for processing

Individuals with ASD process auditory information at a slower rate than typical individuals, yet many times we expect them to respond quickly. Some individuals with ASD may require several seconds or even several minutes before they are able to process and respond to what was said. Given this, caregivers and professionals must be willing to allow extended time for an individual with ASD to process the auditory information.

Case Example
BOBBY

Bobby is an 11-year-old child who was diagnosed with the DSM-IV with PPD-NOS, anxiety disorder, AD/HD, and a written language disorder. When I first began to see Bobby, I quickly realized I was making a lot of mistakes. I would start a session by asking him to tell me about his day. At that point, Bobby would just sit there. After about 10 seconds I would ask Bobby if he understood the question. He would then continue to just sit there. I then repeated the same question to Bobby, "Tell me about your day?" Many times I found myself becoming uncomfortable with the silence, so I would talk again. After several sessions of making these mistakes, I asked him the same question, "Tell me about your day?" and then I sat and waited. I waited three minutes. Three minutes is a long time to sit in silence. After three minutes, Bobby said, "I'm not sure what you want me to tell you." When I asked what he meant, I waited again three minutes. Bobby then told me that he could tell me about his day but that I would likely not want to listen. He continued to tell me that he knows how to answer that question but that his answer was too detailed and I would not approve.

I forgot that Bobby has ASD. I forgot that his brain works differently than mine and that he is only able to attend to one piece of information at a time. Because the part of his brain that is able to process complex information is differnt, he is unable to provide a shortened answer. Bobby then told me that most of the time he tries to guess what people want him to say since he knows his detailed answer is not something they want to hear. I learned a lot in those three minutes of silence. Now Bobby and I have a phrase that we say to each other when it is ok to not follow "social rule." The phrase is "no restrictions." This allows Bobby to know it is ok to swear (which he would never do in front of me unless we say no restrictions) or give detailed answers to my questions. Since then, we rarely sit in silence together.

Provide missing information

If an individual with ASD has missed cues, then you want to provide information that might help explain the situation. First, reinforce others around you for engaging in the correct response. For example, instead of telling Johnny, an individual with ASD, to pick up his pencil, you might instead praise someone else in the room for engaging in the desired behavior, such as saying, "Sally, thanks for picking up your pencil." You can also share your thoughts, feelings, and actions as an example. For example, I might say to Jenny, an individual with ASD, who did not say goodbye to me after a session, "I'm really sad when people forget to say goodbye to me." You can also provide choices that they understand. When providing choices, it is important to only provide two or three choices. For example, if Robert, an individual with ASD, forgot to say hello, I might say, "Would you like to say hello or wave hello to me?"

Make it positive

The key to teaching any type of communication strategy is to make it positive. Many times, we tend to use negative communication with individuals with ASD. Negative communication may be repeating the same question again or even asking the individual with ASD if they understood the question. A better solution is to wait longer for a response and if they do not answer, then rephrase your questions so that it is more concrete. To assist in making the situation more positive, you may wish to try techniques such as incidental teaching. Incidental teaching requires that you set up the environment for success. First, you set up the environment to encourage the individual's interests. Part of your goal is to pair something they like with their environment or task. Then you wait for the individual to show interest in that item. After, prompt a response related to that item. Once they respond appropriately, reward the individual with the actual item or activity. Lastly, fade your prompts until the student responds independently.

SOCIAL COMMUNICATION STRATEGIES

Individuals with ASD have difficulty with social communication and understanding pragmatic language. It is important for every individual with ASD to work with a professional who specializes in teaching pragmatic language and social communication skills. Professionals such as speech language pathologists, counselors, or psychologists can be extremely helpful in teaching these skills.

Social skills training programs

There have been numerous studies that have been conducted on social skills training programs. Most of the studies demonstrate that there is limited effectiveness in social skills training programs for children with ASD (Bellini, Peters, Benner, Hopf, 2007; Cappadocia & Weiss, 2011). This is because most individuals with ASD have difficulty generalizing the social skills they learn from one situation to another. In a review of several studies, typically the maintenance effects of social skills instructions was moderately strong, meaning the individual could learn the skill, they only had difficulty applying the skill to other settings. Social skills intervention programs were most effective for middle and high school age students. Elementary school children showed the lowest intervention and generalization effects, while preschool age children demonstrated the lowest maintenance effects. The social skills interventions in the general classroom showed significantly stronger intervention, maintenance, and generalization effects than social skills interventions delivered in pull-out programs.

Those who have reviewed skills training programs (Reichow and Volkmar, 2010) have identified certain aspects of social skills training programs that have demonstrated the most positive intervention effects. Such interventions are those that are based on techniques using ABA. With younger children, those social skills training programs that used naturalistic techniques and parent training were most effective. Those social skills training programs that also used peer training showed positive effects, as well as those social skills training programs that used visual supports and video modeling.

■ *Social Skills Group Example*

If your only option is to use a pull-out social skills program, here is a model we created that incorporates many research-based strategies:

1. A token economy is set up, where group participants earn tokens to trade in for the token box or vending machine. We use a five-token and a 10-token reward system.

2. Group participants are allowed to interact in a fun group environment, which contains interactive games, such as ping pong, air hockey, basketball, foosball, and various board games. Staff reinforce with tokens and model appropriate social skills.

3. Group participants sit down and receive a visual handout that details the skill they will be practicing during group.

4. Group participants learn and practice the skill through role-play, social stories, video-monitoring, and other visual techniques.

5. Group participants return to the fun group environment, practicing the skills learned in a more natural environment.

6. Parents and caregivers are asked to attend the last 5 to 10 minutes of the session, where they receive a handout of the skill learned and how they can practice the skill with their child or young adult at home.

7. Participants give the parents a sort of "show and tell" of the skill learned.

8. Participants are given a skill chart, where they are to record every time they have practiced the skill. Parents are encouraged to share this skill chart and other handouts with the participants' teachers or bosses, so that they can also practice the skill in either the school or work environment.

9. Age-appropriate peers are invited to volunteer and participate in the groups as much as possible.

Lunch bunches

A "Lunch Bunch" is typically a technique used within the school system. It entails a social skills class during lunch time. It is important to understand the target behavior for the individual with ASD during this Lunch Bunch activity. If the goal for this individual is to work on social skills, then it is important to have the social skills class in an environment other than the lunch room. If the individual has gained appropriate social skills and the next goal is for them to be exposed to the lunch environment, then it is important to gradually expose the individual to the lunch room. For example, the first day you may just walk with that individual by the lunch room. The second day may include walking into the lunch room for three seconds and then walking out of the lunch room. On the third day, you may just walk into the lunch room and point to the lunch table where you and the student will sit the next day. The fourth day may include walking into the lunch room and then sitting at the lunch table for a couple seconds. The goal is to set the individual with ASD up for success. The lunch room is typically an extremely loud and unstructured setting that is very difficult for an individual with ASD to sit in. Given this, it is important to remember that if the goal is to teach social skills, then that is best done in a quiet environment away from the lunch room.

Video modeling

Video modeling can be a great visual tool to assist the individual with ASD to understand social skills and what is not appropriate. It is important when using video modeling that you record both the individual with ASD as well as another individual, such as a peer. If you use video modeling of the individual with ASD alone, many times this approach may not be effective. This is because the individual with ASD may observe nothing wrong in watching themselves. When they see themselves, they often do not see anything wrong, as they are viewing what they have already defined as appropriate within themselves. If they see another individual perform that same skill in which they have no definition of that individual, then they may recognize what is and is not appropriate.

Social stories™

Social stories include short stories that are created to educate, teach, and reflect upon social situations (Gray, 2010). Carol Gray also created comic strip conversations, which are similar to social stories with the difference that they rely on the participation of the child in creating them (Gray, 1994). Social stories are widely used with the ASD population and are often integrated into a behavioral program. Although case studies have shown social stories and comic strip conversations to be promising interventions with the ASD population (Hutchins & Prelock, 2006), further research is needed to explore the efficacy of these alternative methods of ASD treatment.

Case Example
JOEY

Joey is an 11-year-old boy with level one ASD who has gotten into the habit of wearing his pants above his belly button. At school, many of the kids begin to tease Joey for wearing his pants that way. In therapy sessions, video modeling was used so that Joey could see what he looked like with his pants above his bellybutton, as well as his pants below his belly button. Joey was unable to recognize what was wrong with seeing his pants above his belly button.

Wearing his pants above his belly button was part of Joey's definition of what he looked like. Therefore, he did not look silly. Taking this exercise a step further, I decided to retrieve Joey from the waiting room with my pants pulled up above my belly button. Joey, as well as the 10 other people in the waiting room, laughed uncontrollably. Once Joey was taken back into my office, a video was taken of me wearing my pants above my bellybutton, as well as below the belly button. When Joey observed me with my pants above my belly button, Joey laughed hysterically. He then understood that it was quite silly for Dr. Daily to wear her pants above her belly button. Joey never wore his pants above his belly button again.

■ *Social Story™ Example*

Saying Hello

There are many ways to say hello to someone.

When I see someone I know, usually I will look at them, smile, and say, "hi," or "hello." They may say, "hello" back. They may stop to talk with me.

Sometimes I will try to shake their hand. Sometimes, when I am visiting a relative or a close friend, I will try to give them a small hug or a little pat on the back or the shoulder.

Sometimes, if I am just passing someone I know, I smile, wave, or just nod. Most people like it when I smile at them. Smiling can make people feel good.

Many times social stories can be more effective if they are constructed along with the individual with ASD. When constructing the social story with the individual, it is important to ask them questions that they can readily answer.

Case Example

RALPH

Ralph is a six-year-old boy diagnosed with level one ASD. His mom brought him into a session, reporting that Ralph is having extreme difficulty sharing and taking turns. Mom described Ralph refusing to play with others; he only wanted to play with his own toys. When others approached him, Ralph would yell at them if they tried to play with what he wanted to play with. At that time, the therapist asked Ralph if he would like to write a story on the computer about taking turns. Ralph was excited about writing a social story and asked if he could name the title of the book "Ninja Turtles." Of course, he could use the title, "Ninja Turtles," but the story also had to focus on taking turns. Ralph was ok with that.

He sat down at the computer with the therapist and the therapist began asking Ralph questions. First, she asked Ralph, "When should we take turns?" Ralph quickly responded, "When I play with my brother and my friends." The therapist praised Ralph and asked if she could use those exact words in the story. She then typed it in. Next, she asked Ralph, "What happens when you take turns?" Ralph again correctly answered, "People may like me more." This type of questioning continued throughout the session. Ralph even got to add his own flare to the story about his interests in birds and ninja turtles. They added pictures to the story and changed the font to what Ralph desired. He was so proud of his story, he read it to mom and then to dad once he got home. They then read it every night together until the next session.

■ *Social Story Example*

Ninja Turtles

Taking turns is important when playing with my brother and my friends.

People may like me more when I take turns.

You have to let someone else have a turn when talking or playing.

I like to play birds and ninja turtles. Sometimes other kids like to play with other toys. I need to remember to take turns and play with what they want to play with first. For example, I don't always like to play superman, but if my friend wanted to, I should do it. Afterward, we can take turns and maybe play with what I want to play with.

When I take turns with my friends, they may like me more. If I learn to take turns with other kids, I will make more friends.

Taking turns is good.

I have also found it quite helpful to use social stories with adults. Since actually constructing a social story as an adult may seem beneath them, it is quite useful to use an adult with ASD to help construct social stories for younger individuals with ASD.

Social stories can also be used with lower functioning individuals who have level three ASD. When using social stories with lower functioning individuals, it is important to use as many visuals as possible. It is now quite easy to create a social story using visual cue cards from online programs, such as Boardmaker®. There are also specific apps and programs that allow for pictures of the actual child to be incorporated into the social story.

Sometimes, the most difficult skills to teach individuals with ASD are those related to hygiene, sex, and masturbation. This is especially difficult with a lower functioning individual. When tackling these sometimes uncomfortable topics, it is important to remember that the individual with ASD has difficulty understanding abstract concepts. Each of these topics requires larger concepts that are difficult for an individual with ASD to process. It is important to help them understand these concepts by breaking them down into extremely small steps. Many times, if they don't understand a concept that is also self-stimulating, the individual may sometimes perseverate even more on the topics and engage in those activities more frequently than a typical individual.

Case Example
CARRIE

Carrie is a 19-year-old female with level two ASD. Despite years of interventions and working on social skills, Carrie still has difficulty greeting others. Carrie has done social stories in the past when she was younger, but never generalized the skill to the actual social setting. One day in a therapeutic session, she was asked if she would like to create social stories for the 3-to-5-year-old social skills class. The topic was on how to say hello to someone. Carrie was extremely excited for the opportunity to help and created five social stories within the hour. All the stories were appropriate for 3-to-5-year-olds and she even drew pictures on each social story. Next, Carrie asked if she could come to the 3-to-5-year-old social skills group to teach her social stories. When asked if she would also role-play those social stories with the 3-to-5-year-olds, Carrie happily replied, "Of course!" The next week Carrie attended the 3-to-5-year-old social skills class and individually taught each child the social story and role-played how to say hello with them. A week later, Carrie began to say hello to everyone in our office when she arrived.

Case Example
ROBBIE

Robbie is a 15-year-old male who has a moderate intellectual disability, is nonverbal, and is diagnosed with level three ASD. Robbie has begun to masturbate in public several times a day. Robbie's caregivers and professionals have found it very difficult to not provide attention to Robbie when he begins to masturbate in public. The use of a visual-based social story was extremely helpful in reducing masturbation in public. First, the antecedent to masturbation was identified. For Robbie, the antecedent was that he would put his finger in his anus and then smell it. When this occurred, no verbal attention was provided to Robbie. Instead, hand sanitizer was applied to his hands and he was taught to point to or give a visual bathroom card to whomever he was with. Once in the bathroom, a visual schedule of how to masturbate in a timely manner was provided with a timer of five minutes. Each visual picture broke down the steps, such as pull down your pants, sit on the toilet, touch your penis, wait for the timer, pull your pants up, flush the toilet, wash your hands, and exit the room. After two weeks of this intervention, Robbie finally learned where it was appropriate to touch himself and he began to only masturbate in the bathroom. Going to the bathroom was already on his visual schedule throughout the day, so it was an easy transition for him to learn that the bathroom is an appropriate place to masturbate.

Social autopsies

A social autopsy is a technique created by Rick Lavoie (as cited in Bieber, 1994). It is a technique used to help individuals with ASD identify the mistake or social error that they have made. Most individuals with ASD have extreme difficulty admitting they have made a mistake. This is not because they are defiant. It is because they perceive that they are correct in the social situation, based on their definition of social rules. This is why it is important for them to understand that their definition of a specific social rule and another person's definition of that same social rule may be different. A social autopsy also involves practicing this skill through role-play, video monitoring, and social stories. The therapist also provides homework for the individual with ASD to practice the skill. I like to think of a social autopsy as a cognitive behavioral strategy for identifying mistakes individuals have made. **A sample social autopsy worksheet is included at the end of the chapter**.

Steps of a social autopsy

1. Ask person to explain what happened.
2. Ask person to identify the mistake(s) that was made.
3. Assist person in determining the actual social error that was made and teach more appropriate responses.
4. Practice the skills
   - Role Play
   - Video
   - Create Social Story/Comic Strip
5. Provide social homework.

I have found one of the hardest tasks in performing a social autopsy with an individual with ASD is step three, assisting the person in determining the actual social error that was made. In the past, I have found that these conversations can many times lead to arguments. As a result, I have created my own technique that has been helpful in having individuals with ASD recognize that they made a mistake. It involves breaking down the actual situation step-by-step and then providing a concrete object in visual form, so that they can understand who has made mistakes in the situation. The following case example demonstrates the technique.

Case Example

ADAM

Adam is an eight-year-old boy with level one ASD. He presented in my office because he was in trouble for pushing a girl at recess. When I asked Adam what had happened, he told me he did nothing wrong and that this girl named Amy had started it. To help Adam realize that it was ok to give me every detail of what happened, I told him to pretend that there was a video camera at recess. I then asked him to tell me exactly what happened, based on what the video camera recorded. As a result, Adam begins to tell me that Amy called him "a loser" and therefore she was to blame. At this point, I had taken a box of blocks, which I placed on the table, and told Adam I wanted to play a game. Many individuals with ASD can be quite competitive and like to win at games. I told Adam that, in order to win this game, he had to have the least amount of blocks at the end of the story. I told him to tell me what was happening in the video again. Adam began to give me every detail. First, he told me Amy called him a mean name. In response, I said, "Amy was wrong. You were right, Adam. Amy did start the fight. Amy gets one block. Look, Adam, you're winning the game right now. You have the least amount of blocks. Okay, Adam, what happens next?" Adam replies, "Well. . . I pushed her." I responded, "Oh. . .sorry Adam. Any type of physical aggression is two blocks. So, here's your two blocks. Now, what happened next?" "Amy pushed me back," replied Adam. "Amy got two more blocks. Amy's losing the game. Alright, Adam what happened next?" Adam stated with his head down, "I kicked Amy." I gave Adam two more blocks and asked, "Then what happened?" Adam responded that the aide intervened and took them both inside.

As I processed this activity with Adam, we discussed that I agreed with him that Amy was wrong and she started it, but at the end of the social situation I asked, "Who had more blocks? You or Amy?" Adam then quietly said, "I did." "So who lost the game?" Adam quietly responded, "I did." I then worked with Adam on creating more appropriate responses to communicate with Amy when he was at recess.

We created a social story and took a video of us role-playing different social scenarios. I then wrote down his coping skills on a visual card so that he could practice them a home. I also gave a copy to his teacher and asked the teacher just to point to the visual card before he left for recess each day. I didn't want the teacher to talk with him about it as he would likely not process verbal communication before going to recess. Interestingly enough, a couple months later, Adam came in and he had gotten into trouble for something at home. He initially had a hard time admitting that he did something wrong, until I got the box of blocks out. He looked at me and quickly said with sort of a scowl, "Alright, I was wrong to hit my brother. I get it." Adam wasn't happy about it, but he realized that he knew he did something wrong, even if he did not start it.

The following worksheets were created at Daily Behavioral Health (2007-2015) with the assistance of other psychologists, educators, and psychology trainees. They can be used individually or in group settings.

1) ***Social Autopsy*** is a great tool to use to assist individuals with ASD to break down the social situation and to identify mistakes they might have made.

2) ***My Privacy Circle.*** Privacy circles, also knows as friendship circles, are a visual method to help individuals with ASD identify people in their lives who may be friends, acquaintances, or strangers.

3) ***Protect Personal Space.*** Educating the individual with ASD about personal space is important. This worksheet identifies five types of personal space: body, property, sound, sight, and thought.

4) ***Expanding My Interests.*** Many times, individuals with ASD are very focused on their own interests and have a difficult time thinking about what others may be interested in. This worksheet helps the individual think about strategies to expand their interests.

5) ***Voice Volumes.*** Recognizing when to use appropriate voice tone and volume are sometimes difficult for an individual with ASD. This worksheet provides sample situations and asks the individual to identify what type of voice volume should be used (e.g., none, soft, normal, or loud).

6) ***Hello.*** To help individuals with ASD remember the rules for saying hello to someone, a mnemonic device using the letters for HELLO (e.g., **H**ello, **E**xpression, **L**ook, **L**isten, **O**n topic) is provided. Individuals are then asked to write a social story to remember these important steps in saying hello.

7) ***Body Languages.*** Understanding nonverbal communication is a challenge for many individuals with ASD. This worksheet provides real-life pictures of children who are expressing themselves using body language. Individuals must then check the box that best fits what they are "saying" with their body language.

Worksheet
Social Autopsy

Directions: Describe what happened by answering the following questions.

NAME: _____ DATE: _____

Situation:

When did it happen?

Where were you?

Who was involved?

What happened that was negative?

What mistake did you make?

What could you have done differently?

How can you practice what you should do differently?

Sam's Privacy Circle

Directions: Write down names of people who are in your privacy circle.

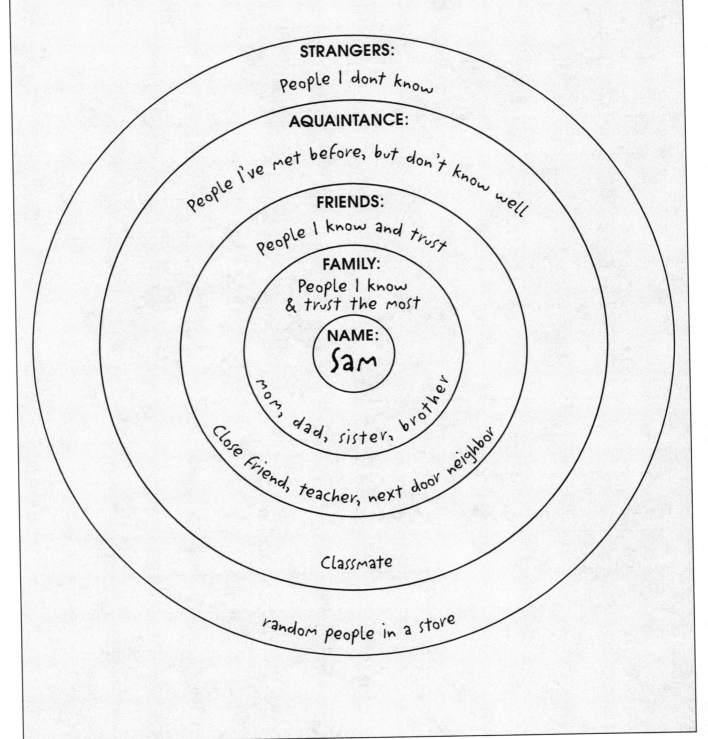

STRANGERS:
People I dont know

AQUAINTANCE:
People I've met before, but don't know well

FRIENDS:
People I know and trust

FAMILY:
People I know
& trust the most

NAME:
Sam

mom, dad, sister, brother

Close friend, teacher, next door neighbor

Classmate

random people in a store

Worksheet

My Privacy Circle

Directions: Write down names of people who are in your privacy circle.

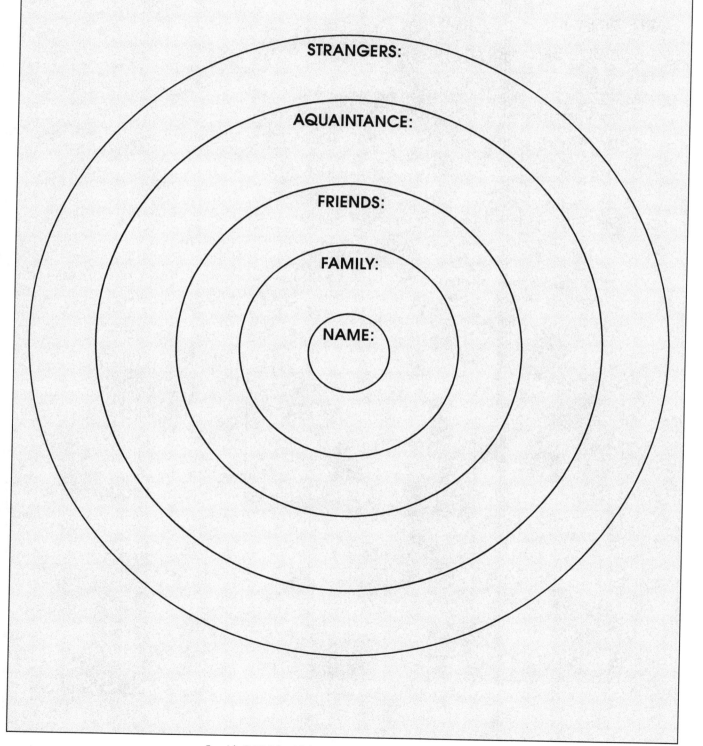

STRANGERS:

AQUAINTANCE:

FRIENDS:

FAMILY:

NAME:

Protect Personal Space

Directions: Circle the pictures that protect personal space.

TYPES OF SPACE:

<u>BODY SPACE</u> - Keep appropriate distance. One arm's length away. *Don't get too close or touch too much.*

<u>PROPERTY SPACE</u> - Keep your hands on our own work and things. *Don't touch things that belong to others and listen when told not to touch something.*

<u>SOUND SPACE</u> - Talk when appropriate and at the right volume. *Don't continue to talk when people tell you to stop, don't talk at the wrong time, and don't talk too loud or too soft.*

<u>SIGHT SPACE</u> - Show things to people at an appropriate distance. *Don't hold objects too close or too far away from someone's face.*

<u>THOUGHT SPACE</u> - Show appropriate respect for others thoughts, feelings, and beliefs. *Think before you say something. Don't be inconsiderate of others feelings, and don't belittle their opinions or beliefs.*

Expanding My Interests

People have different interests. Some people like different movies and TV shows. Some people like to play different games and sports. Some people like to talk about different subjects. It's important to have several interests. How do you expand your interests? Here are some tips to help:

1. First of all, it helps to know what others your age like doing or talking about.

   • Ask your friends and others what they like doing or playing. You can also watch to see what they do.

2. When you have found out what others like doing, try it out.

   • For example, if your friends like playing basketball, you can practice at home. Then ask if you can play basketball with them at recess.

3. If you have trouble finding people who do things that look like fun, try to find things in your community or online that might be fun.

   • Check out things at the community recreation centers, after-school activities, or clubs. You can usually find sports teams, chess clubs, computer game conventions, or other things you would like to try. Keep your eyes open and look for things. If you find something you are interested in, you are likely to find people who you will like spending time with, too.

4. Remember, most things are not fun until you have tried them for a while.

   • For example, if you love Superman and know everything about him, it's going to take time before you know as much about football, and like it as much.

5. Remember, you have nothing to lose by trying new things.

   • If you don't like an activity after trying it, you can try something else. Try new activities at least three times before giving up. If you don't like the new thing as much, you may still find a new friend, which will make it worthwhile.

6. Trying new things and learning about them can be hard, but the good things are:

   • You can find something new to do that is more fun than what you used to do!

   • You can learn new things.

   • You can make new friends who also like your new interests!

   • The more things you know about and like to do, the more fun you will have.

   • And more kids will want to play with you!

Help Others Expand their Interests by Writing a Letter

Directions: The following are examples of letters written by other children who need your help to expand their interests. Read each letter and fill in the blanks.

Hello everybody! My name is Joseph. I love playing with my action figures, and I had a best friend in school that I used to play with all the time. We would bring our action figures for recess and talk about them a lot. My problem is that my friend just moved and changed schools, and now I don't have anyone to play with. All of the other kids are just playing on the monkey bars or playing basketball – things that I have never done. What should I do?

Dear Joseph,
You should try to learn what others are doing at recess. An activity I enjoy doing at recess is_____ .

Hi. My name is Michael. I have a problem I am hoping you can help me with. Last year my classmates and I used to play tag at recess. I loved it and wanted to do it all the time. This year, it seems like no one but me wants to do that anymore. I would like to play with my classmates, but I don't know what to do.

Dear Michael,
An activity you and your friends may enjoy is_____.
I also like to play _____ at recess.

Hi everyone! My name is Allison. I love dogs and know almost everything about them. I know the names of a lot of different kinds of dogs and I can draw them really well. My room at home is filled with stuffed animals - mostly dogs - who I have named. My problem is that now in school, no one wants to listen when I tell them about dogs. What can I do?

Dear Allison,
You should ask your friends about what they like. Maybe they like to talk about something else, such as _____ .
Sometimes I have to talk about _____ with my friends, even though I don't always like to talk about it.

Worksheet
Voice Volume

Directions: Mark the appropriate box for an individual's voice volume during each situation.

	None	Soft	Normal	Loud
Playing a video game	☐	☐	☐	☐
At study hall	☐	☐	☐	☐
In the gym	☐	☐	☐	☐
At a funeral	☐	☐	☐	☐
Playing at the pool	☐	☐	☐	☐
Doing homework	☐	☐	☐	☐
At the library	☐	☐	☐	☐
In a doctor's waiting room	☐	☐	☐	☐
Eating in a resturant	☐	☐	☐	☐
Watching a movie	☐	☐	☐	☐
Taking a test	☐	☐	☐	☐
Playing outside	☐	☐	☐	☐
At a party	☐	☐	☐	☐
Talking in class	☐	☐	☐	☐
Riding in the car	☐	☐	☐	☐
Cheering for a sports team	☐	☐	☐	☐
At a museum	☐	☐	☐	☐
When a teacher is talking	☐	☐	☐	☐

Worksheet
Hello

Directions: Create a social story about saying Hello to someone at school or at home. Use the following five words and/or phrases in the story: hello, expression, look, listen, and on topic.

Hello or Hi – When you see someone you know, start by saying **Hello** or Hi.

Expression – Most people smile at the person they see when they say Hello. Check your facial **expression** to see if you are smiling when you say Hello.

Look – It is important to **look** at the person when you say Hello so they know you are talking to them. You should try to look toward their face.

Listen – After you say Hello, **listen** to what the person is saying to you.

On Topic – If the person begins to talk about a certain topic, stay **on topic** by talking about the same subject.

_____

_____

_____

_____

_____

_____

_____

_____

_____

_____

_____

_____

_____

Worksheet
Body Language

Directions: Check the box that best fits what these people are "saying" with their body language.

Did you know that you are talking to people not just by your words, but also by your tone of voice, your body language and your facial expressions? For example, if you say "sorry" but your face still looks angry and you turn away from the other person, do you think that they are going to believe that you are really sorry? Let's practice understanding body language.

It's a rainy day and Tommy is stuck inside.
Do you think he is …

☐ Excited
☐ Bored
☐ Angry

Mark's mother just told him some news.
Do you think the news is …

☐ Good
☐ Interesting
☐ Bad

Shelby just opened a gift.
Do you think she looks …

☐ Sad
☐ Excited
☐ Tired

From the look on his face, Charlie must feel ...

☐ Angry
☐ Disappointed
☐ Suprised

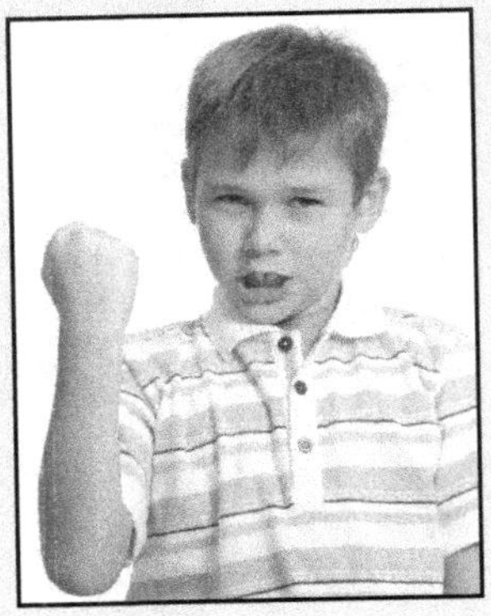

Dillion was just put in time out.

Do you think he feels ...

☐ Mad
☐ Excited
☐ Disappointed

How do you think Michelle feels about her puppy?
Is she ...

☐ Angry at her puppy
☐ Loving her puppy
☐ Disgusted with her puppy

Does Amanda feel ...

☐ Sad
☐ Surprised
☐ Irritable

Chapter EIGHT

Environmental Strategies

ORGANIZATIONAL SYSTEMS

Certain environmental strategies can be very helpful to an individual with ASD. For example, color coordinating folders for certain subjects can be helpful. Creating a visual organization system at home, so they know where to put their coat, shoes, toys, and so forth, can eliminate a lot of repetitive verbal communication. Using a PECS that labels where each item goes can be beneficial. If it difficult to create numerous PECS, take a picture of an area when it is organized and then put that picture there so that the individual with ASD can reference the picture to assist with organization. This approach may take them longer to process as there may be too many details in the picture, although it more helpful than verbally communicating to them where items should be placed. This approach can also work well in teaching an individual how to organize a desk or locker.

Visual schedules, checklists, and calendars

Organizational systems such as visual schedules, checklists, calendars, timelines, outlines, and picture organizers are also extremely helpful. Some individuals require a detailed visual schedule, whereas others do not. For example, an individual with ASD and OCD would not benefit from a detailed schedule. Instead, they would perform much better with being presented one visual item at a time. In today's world, there are numerous tablets, smart phone, and computer apps that provide visual schedules and checklists. These can be quite helpful for the individual with ASD. I would recommend that, if you are using technology in teaching individuals with ASD, you color coordinate your technology device so that they know when the tablet is being used for work versus play. For example, if the tablet is in the green case, then it is for play. When the tablet is in the blue case, then it is for work. You can also just *Velcro* a visual icon of either work or play to the top of the tablet. This is extremely helpful since, many times, when an individual with ASD sees a tablet, they automatically assume it is a play device. **There are several examples at the end of this chapter.**

Visual schedules

Teaching flexibility to an individual with ASD can be quite challenging. One technique that I have found helpful is to teach flexibility using a visual schedule. A simple way to do this is on their visual daily schedule is to have a "?" at a certain time of the day. Putting a "?" onto their visual schedule allows the individual with ASD to be primed that they will be doing an activity that they may not be prepared for. By priming the individual with ASD, they will be better prepared to cope with the transition and possible unstructured activity. When teaching this concept, it is important to sometimes provide preferred activities during this "?" time, such as watching TV or playing a video game, as well as sometimes a more non-preferred activity such as a worksheet, lining up in a line, or some other type of activity.

Timelines

Visual timelines are also extremely helpful for an individual with ASD to organize larger projects or specific goals. Many times, an individual with ASD believes they can complete a large project the night before since they were able to do a similar project previously on the night before. Therefore, that is the rule for all projects.

A timeline can help break down the larger project into small steps, so that the individual with ASD can see a more realistic goal for the project. It is important to also have accountability for this timeline and to set goals for individuals with ASD to complete tasks at a certain time.

Outlines and picture organizers

In teaching concepts, it is helpful to use a visual organization systems such as Venn and Web diagrams. A Venn diagram can help show the overlapping relationships between certain concepts and can be an effective visual teaching tool for an individual with ASD. Similarly, a web diagram or graphical organizer can help break down steps or parts of a larger concept to help the individual with ASD organize their thoughts. When we work with children, we call them outline or picture organizers. The use of conceptual, hierarchical, cyclical, and sequential graphic organizers can all be helpful.

CLASSROOM MODIFICATIONS

Preferential seating

Given that it is best to teach an individual with ASD at one arm's length away at a 90° angle, it is important to provide preferential or adjusted seating. This should be the case in any type of classroom for a one-on-one setting, except if this situation involves an aide or paraprofessional. If the aid or paraprofessional is not teaching, they should not be sitting that close to the individual with ASD. If that aid or paraprofessional wishes to gain that individuals attention and teach them a specific task, then it is important for them to be at a distance of one arm's length away and at a 90° angle. If an individual with ASD is sitting farther than one arm length away, they will have difficulty processing information.

Minimize transitions

Individuals with ASD have difficulty with unstructured transitions and extraneous sensory stimuli in this environment. It is extremely important to minimize transitions throughout the day. If transitions have to occur, it is important they are quiet, free from extraneous unexpected sensory stimuli, extremely structured, and visual. For example, if during a transition the individual with ASD has to get in a line with other individuals, it would be important to give the individual with ASD a visual picture of where they are going next. This will allow the individual with ASD to be able to visually focus on something as they are trying to cope with the stress of transitioning to the next activity.

Reinforcement menus

Other environmental strategies include the use of reinforcement menus. It is important for a reinforcement menu to be visual. Many times a reinforcement menu may contain a choice board of a couple different reinforcement options. When creating a reinforcement menu, is important to have the individual with ASD help create it. If that individual likes Angry Birds, then use Angry Birds as tokens. With our families, we provide a reinforcement assessment at least once a month, so that we are able to monitor each individual's changing motivators.

Prepare ahead of time

Given that many aspects of the day for an individual with ASD can be quite negative, it is important to set them up for success and opportunities. In order for this to happen, it is important to prepare people, activities, and the environment ahead of time. Once you have prepared everything ahead of time, you must also understand that what you have planned may not be the goal once the individual with ASD arrives. It is extremely important to only be focused on the present time with an individual with ASD. Most individuals with ASD are living in the present and are not focused on the past or what they may have to do in the future. To set them up for the most success, we also need to teach in the present. This requires evaluating their behaviors and mood and teaching according to where they are today.

Priming for changes

Because individuals with ASD have difficulty with changes in their schedule or changes with staff or any type of change, it's imperative to prime them for any type of change. Because their primary language is visual, it's especially important to prime them visually. It is more important to prime them visually and orally. I have many individuals with ASD who have modifications to their schoolwork. Unfortunately, the teacher typically gives the entire class the instructions visually on a piece of paper of what the assignment entails. Then the teacher, parent or intervention specialist orally tells the students with ASD what is different about their assignment. The student with ASD then typically attempts the assignment that the rest of the class was assigned. This is because the modified assignment was not presented visually. Once presented visually, the student with ASD is better able to understand the modification and will be able to follow instructions.

Make sure task is appropriate

If an individual with ASD is struggling with a task, the first step is to verify that the task is appropriate. Just because the individual with ASD could complete that same task the day before, it does not mean the task is appropriate today. There may be some other factor that is interfering with their ability to process the task that we may not be aware of. When an individual with ASD is struggling with a task, it is extremely important to teach them a more appropriate way to ask for help or to take a break from the task or to change the task. Afterward, it is important to make sure the task is appropriate by breaking the steps down into small parts and starting at the simplest part. You should continue to praise and reinforce the individual as they complete the simplest aspects of a task that you know they already know how to do.

Alternating tasks

When working with individuals with ASD, it is extremely important to provide more positive than negative tasks. This is typically because they are receiving much more negative feedback than positive throughout the day. When presenting tasks to an individual with ASD, it is important to alternate preferred tasks with less preferred tasks. If you want to set up an individual with ASD for success, provide five preferred tasks for every less preferred task. This would ensure success for the individual.

Use of base

A safe base or home base is a tool that is extremely effective for an individual with ASD (although I do not see it being used very often). "Home Base" is a technique that was created by Myles & Simpson in 1998. Individuals with ASD have difficulty with unstructured settings and unexpected sensory stimuli. A "base" allows the individual with ASD to have a place to organize their things as well as have a safe place to take a break. A base can be used in a classroom setting or in the workplace.

Instead of using a locker to organize their things, base requires a longer table or a corner in a classroom or work area where an individual with ASD has more room to organize their things. On the table, it is helpful to have visual pictures to help the individual organize their items. For example, there may be several visual pictures on the table that would say "coat," "math book," "homework folder," "lunch," etc. For each item the individual has with them, there should be a visual picture on the desk. In addition, it is helpful to have a chair or a beanbag right next to the table where the individual with ASD knows they can return to home base to take a break from an activity.

Many times it is helpful to have a base card that the individual with ASD can carry with them, so that they can communicate to others when they need a break to go back to base. A timer should be placed somewhere on the table so that, when they request a break at base, they know that they will not be avoiding a task and will need to return to the activity once the timer goes off. Typically 3 to 5 minutes is enough for a break. Given that many of our individuals with ASD have sensory issues, it may also be okay at home base for the child to engage in some sensory stimulation activities such as fidget items that they could also request with the visual card. If you are using a reinforcement system or token system, base is also a place where all of their reinforcement menus, back up reinforcers, and visual schedules can be placed.

Break cards

The use of a break card is considered a positive communication tool. Many times, when I have observed individuals using break cards, it is taught inappropriately. When I have seen it used in the classroom or work environment, it is typically used as a punishment. The individual teaching the child or adult with ASD sees the individual with ASD becoming agitated and therefore prompts that individual by saying, "It looks as if you need a break; go take a break." That is considered punishment. A break card, if it is used appropriately, is meant to teach positive communication.

In order for it to be a form of positive communication, the individual with ASD needs to initiate the use of a break card. In order for that to happen, the individual with ASD has to be a part of the teaching process. First, the individual with ASD should be the one who creates the break card. It doesn't matter if they put their favorite characters on the break card or however they wish to decorate it.

Next, someone needs to teach the individual with ASD how to communicate using the break card. They can raise their hand or match their break card to the break area, or put the brake card on their desk. Involve the individual with ASD in determining where the best place is for the individual to take a break. So, for example, if you are using the method of home base, the individual with ASD can help determine where home base should be and if a chair or bean bag should be used.

It is important to practice using the break card so that the individual understands what will happen and understands that this is a positive communication tool. It's important to practice it at least three times and, each time, use the timer so that the individual knows how long this break time will be. It is also important to establish rules for how many times the break card can be used and for what times of the day. It may be important to write those rules down somewhere on the card or somewhere that is visible to the individual with ASD.

Sample Picture Communication Symbols

Example
Visual Schedule

Directions: Visual schedules can include one visual, 5 visuals, or more than 10 visuals on a schedule. The following can be used for a 5-visual schedule system. It is best to laminate the Visual Schedule, as well as the PECS symbols on the previous page. Cut each PECS symbol, laminate, and then use velcro to attach it to the visual schedule. For example, if the child was to complete the following five tasks: hang up coat, desk work, break, speech therapy, bathroom, then those five symbols would be attached to the card via velcro. To the right of each PECS symbol, the child can then mark off with a check or other symbol when the task is finished. The visual schedule can be modified in several ways to be most effective for each individual child. Sometimes, we have the child "match" PECS symbols for each task so the child knows the task they are working on or put the PECS symbol in a "finished" envelope when the task is completed. It is important to modify the visual schedule to best fit the needs of each child.

Made with Boardmaker® and the Picture Communication Symbols © 1981-2010 Mayer-Johson LLC - 2100 Wharton St. Suite 400. Pittsburgh, PA 15203 U.S.A. Phone (800)588-4548. www.mayer-johson.com

Worksheet
Visual Schedule

Directions: Draw, write or use PECS symbols to show five tasks you want to complete. Check the box when you have completed the task.

Example
Reinforcement Menu

Directions: For most children, it is important to have a reinforcement menu that is displayed where they are working. The following is an example of a five-token economy reinforcement menu. At the bottom of the page, attach three PECS that are reinforcement items for the individual (e.g., tablet, snack, activity). Some individuals respond better if you have a visual symbol of the exact reinforcer (e.g., specific cookie brand). At the beginning of each task, ask the individual what reinforcer they want to work for during the task. If they desire to work for the tablet, then they would place the visual of the tablet in the box after "I am working for". Then use five laminated "tokens" that can be put on the token board as the child is working. Sample tokens of five pennies are included. If the child likes a certain cartoon character or superhero, it is great to just print and laminate that character to use as tokens, too. Depending upon the level of the child, you may reinforce the child quickly with tokens for target behaviors or after completing certain parts of each task. Remember to always use positive descriptive praise (e.g., "Nice matching colors.") when you provide the token.

Made with Boardmaker® and the Picture Communication Symbols © 1981-2010 Mayer-Johnson LLC - 2100 Wharton St. Suite 400. Pittsburgh, PA 15203 U.S.A. Phone (800)588-4548. www.mayer-johson.com

Worksheet
Reinforcement Menu

Directions: Cut out each box around the dotted lines. Label, draw, or attach a picture to the three reinforcement boxes for the child to choose what they will be working for. Laminate each box and use two-sided Velcro to attach the pennies and reinforcement boxes to the token board.

I am working for

Hierarchical Graphic Organizer

Several types of graphic organizers have been included for your use. A hierarchical graphic organizer is great to use when the individual needs to break down a main idea into several details. Conceptual organizers are used in the same way. These types of organizers can be used for simple concepts, such as labeling types of dinosaurs (e.g., Main Idea = Dinosaur; Detail 1 = T-Rex; Detail 2 = Brontosaurus) to more complex concepts, such describing details of a specific type of snake (e.g., Main Idea = Northern Copperhead Rattle Snake; Detail 1 = Eats mice; Detail 2 = Lives in rainy, dark areas). Cyclical and sequential organizers have also been included to help break down concepts that may be based on continuing concepts (e.g., explaining the cyclical nature of the seasons, which include summer, fall, winter, and spring) or time-lines of events (e.g., Time line of major wars).

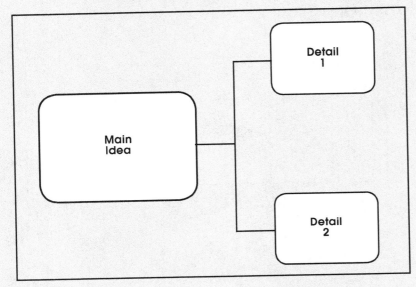

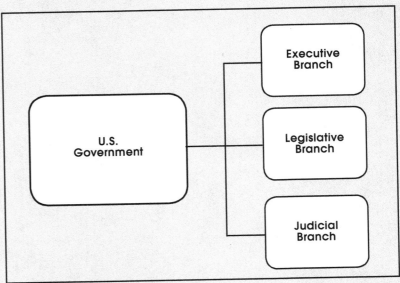

Made with Boardmaker® and the Picture Communication Symbols © 1981-2010 Mayer-Johson LLC - 2100 Wharton St. Suite 400. Pittsburgh, PA 15203 U.S.A. Phone (800)588-4548. www.mayer-johson.com

Worksheet
Hierarchical Graphic Organizer

Directions: Write or draw the main idea in the large box and details in the smaller boxes. Add boxes as needed.

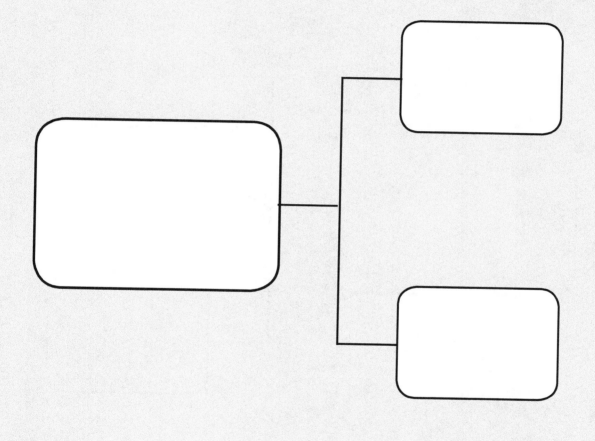

Hierarchical Graphic Organizer

Directions: Write or draw the main idea in the large box and details in the smaller boxes. Add boxes as needed.

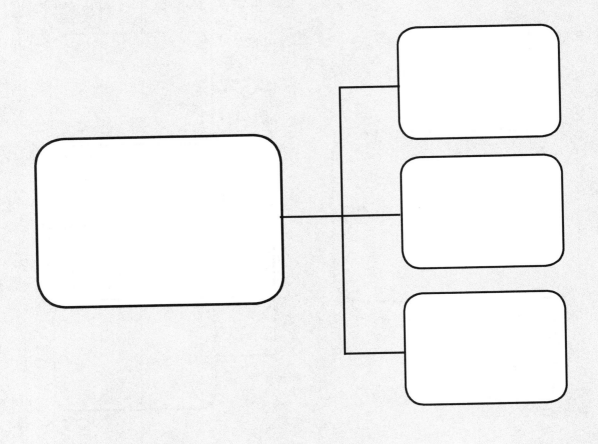

Hierarchical Graphic Organizer

Directions: Write or draw the main idea in the large box and details in the smaller boxes. Add boxes as needed.

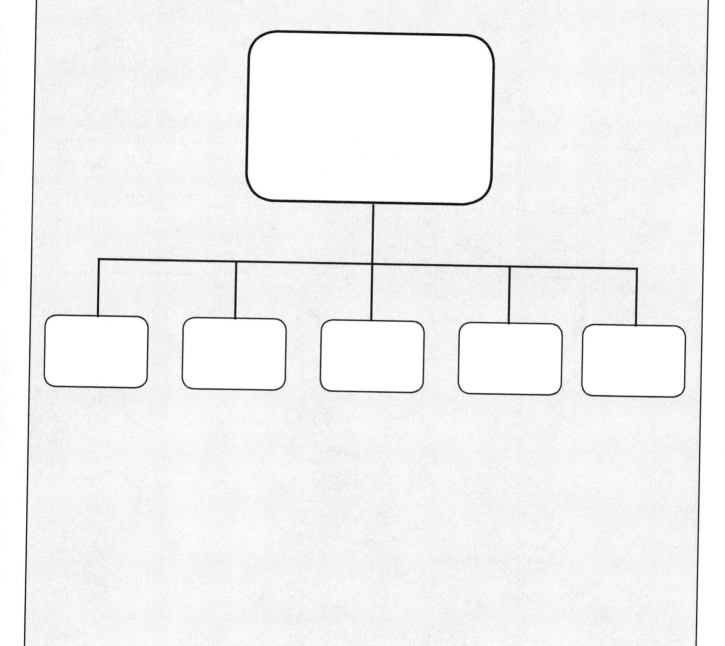

Example
Cyclical Graphic Organizer — Five Steps

Directions: Write each step in a box. Example: Life Cycle of an Apple.

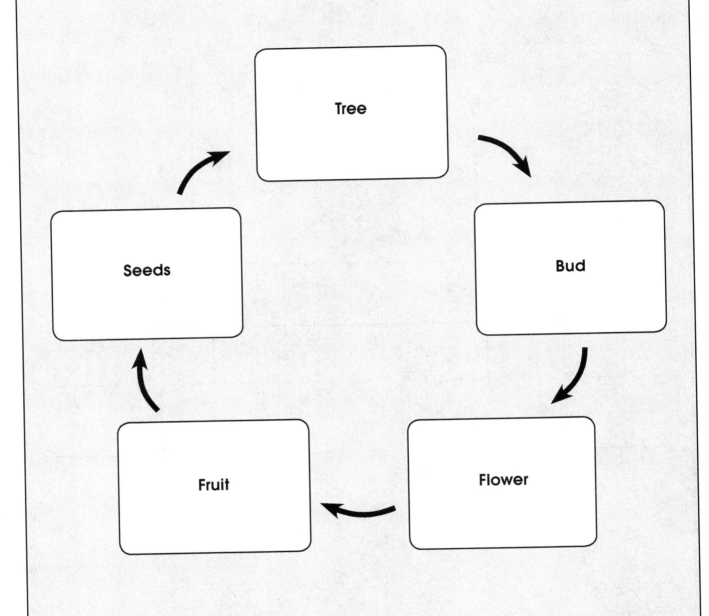

Worksheet
Cyclical Graphic Organizer — Five Steps

Directions: Write each step in a box.

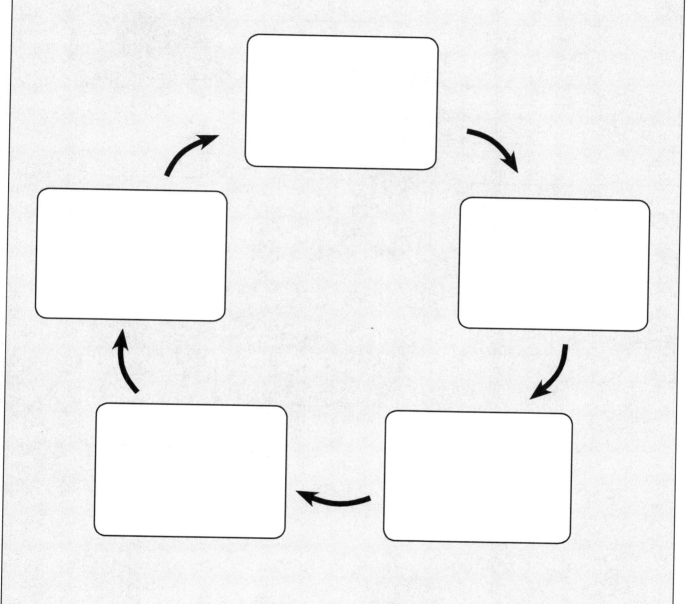

Worksheet
Cyclical Graphic Organizer — Eight Steps

Directions: Write each step in a box.

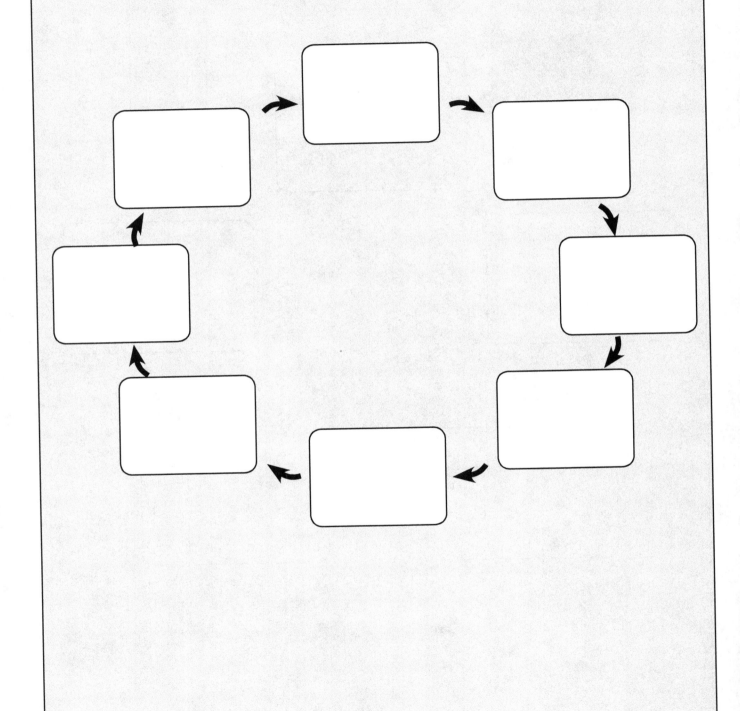

Conceptual Graphic Organizer — Five Details

Directions: Write the main idea in the large box and details in the smaller boxes. Add boxes as needed.
Example: 5 W's

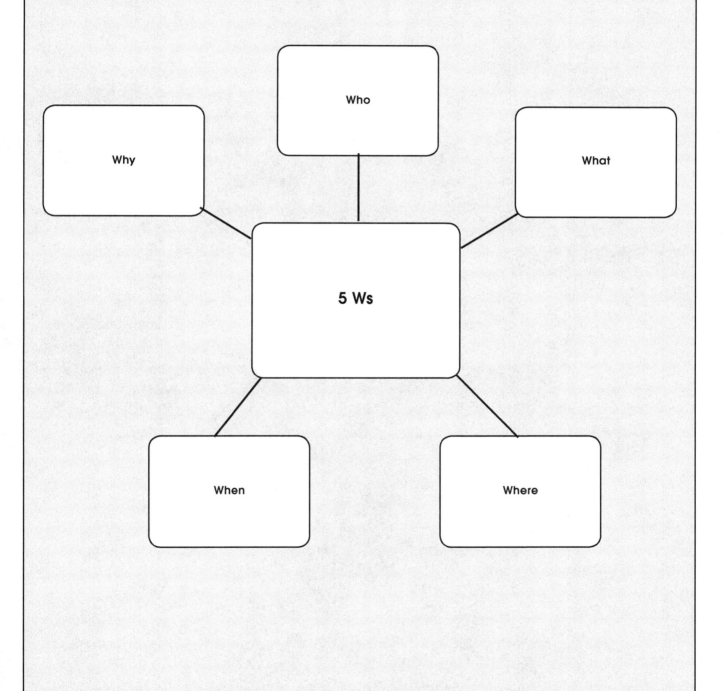

Worksheet
Conceptual Graphic Organizer — Five Details

Directions: Write the main idea in the large box and details in the smaller boxes. Add boxes as needed.

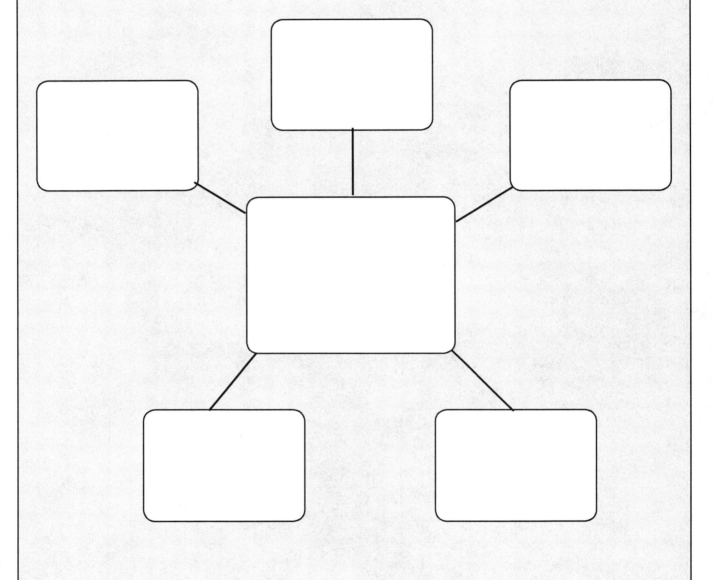

Worksheet
Conceptual Graphic Organizer

Directions: Write the main idea in the large box and details in the smaller boxes. Add boxes as needed.

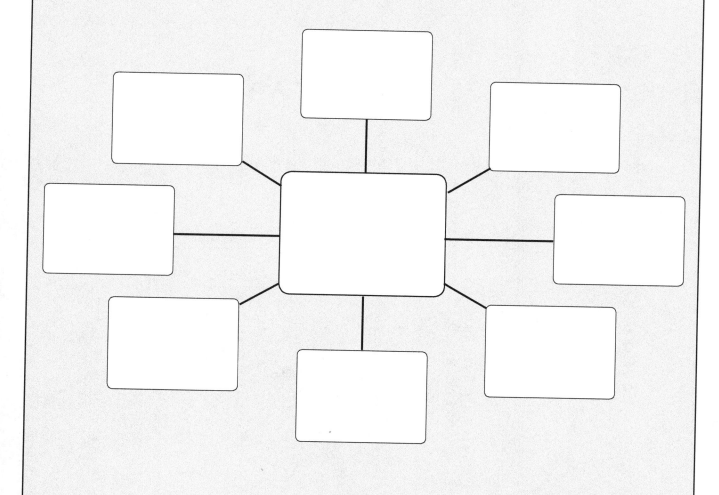

Example

Sequential Graphic Organizer

Directions: Write the sequence of in the white boxes. Add boxes as needed. Example: Timeline of major wars.

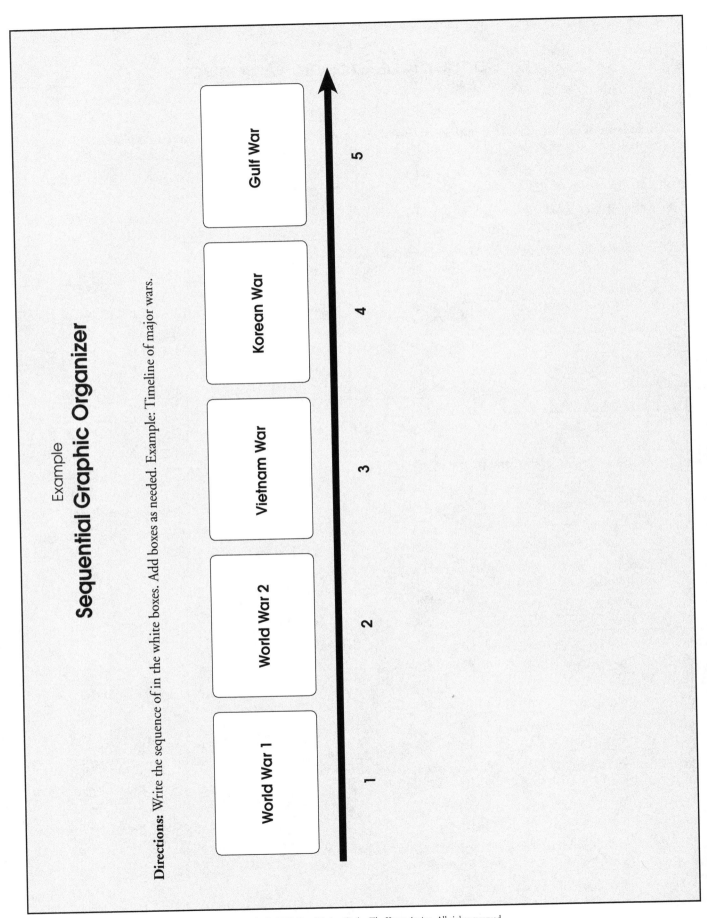

World War 1	World War 2	Vietnam War	Korean War	Gulf War
1	2	3	4	5

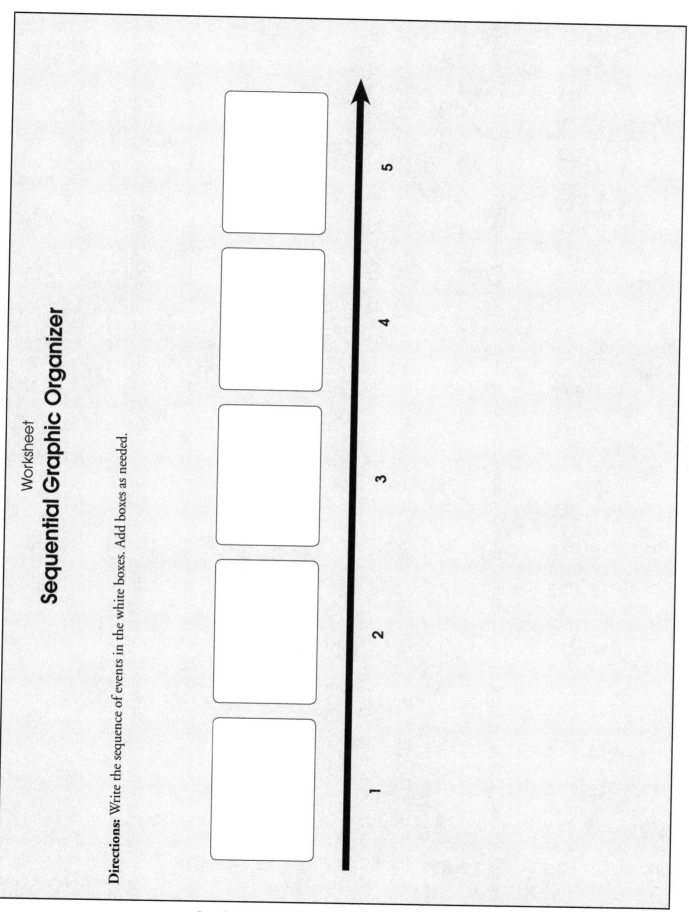

Worksheet

Sequential Graphic Organizer

Directions: Write the sequence of events in the white boxes. Add boxes as needed.

Chapter NINE

Self-Regulation Strategies

Teaching emotional self-regulation can be difficult with an individual with ASD. Self-regulation is the ability to calm oneself when upset. Self-regulation strategies require the understanding of certain concepts, such as feeling words like happy, stressed, or angry. Given that an individual with ASD has difficulty understanding these concepts, it can take months to teach. These are strategies that are typically used with higher functioning individuals with ASD.

EMOTIONAL AND THOUGHT SELF-REGULATION

Understanding emotions

We know recognizing emotions for individuals with autism can be difficult (Uljarvic & Hamilton, 2013). Many times, when teaching a concept, such as happy, an individual with ASD may have over 100 different definitions of what it means for them to be happy. For example, I smiled when I was happy yesterday, but the day before, when I was happy, I clapped my hands. Many times, they can associate one specific behavior with being happy, but have a hard time categorizing all the behaviors together that could mean being happy such as smiling, feeling light, clapping, giggling, laughing, and my voice getting higher. First, the individual with ASD must be able to identify and monitor their emotions before you can teach them self-regulation strategies.

To be able to identify emotions, we must first educate the individual with ASD about emotions using lots of different visuals. Have them use a mirror and ask them to think about something that makes them happy. Then have them see what they look like at that time. Take a picture, record on video, and/or role play various emotions. Have the individual identify and list all the ways a person could look when feeling each emotion. Show the individual visuals of what others look like when they feel a certain emotion. There are a ton of visuals and pictures used to define emotions for ASD on the web and in various books.

Next, expose the individual to visual media (e.g., books, social stories, apps, etc.) that can teach them about emotions. After they are able to recognize emotions in themselves and others, then have them began to monitor and track their emotions. You can give them homework to practice once a day where they track how they feel and why. **A sample emotion tracking sheet is included at the end of this chapter.** The next step would be to teach them to communicate their feelings by using "I feel" statements. **A sample "I feel" worksheet is included.**

Identifying the situation

Many times an individual with ASD can identify the situation that made them upset, but they may have a difficult time communicating the situation to others. I use a simple verbal technique (if the individual is verbal) of asking the individual to imagine having a video camera and to then describe each picture frame that they see in the situation. If they are older and like to draw, have them draw the situation. The goal is to have them "think in pictures" of the situation and then communicate that situation, either verbally or visually (e.g., writing it down, or making a picture).

Changing thought patterns

A common technique used in self-regulation and cognitive-behavioral therapy is to assist the individual in identifying their cognitive distortions and then changing the thought to be more rational. Everyone has distorted thinking patterns, whether they have ASD or not. There are several wonderful treatment program manuals and workbooks. Most programs and books incorporate educating the individual about negative thinking patterns, having them identify their negative thoughts through a thought chart, and then having the individual change the thought to something more positive or rational. Aaron Beck (1967) was one of the first to define cognitive distortions and his student, David Burns, continued his research and published the *Feeling Good Handbook* (1999), which defined cognitive distortions and how to change them. The original handbook is for adults, but many professionals have adapted the content to work with children.

■ *Steps to change distorted thinking patterns*

1. Normalize that everyone engages in negative or distorted thinking. Let him or her know that there are several different words that are used to identify a cognitive distortion, such as twisted thinking, negative thinking, distorted thinking, irrational thinking, and so on. Ask the individual what he/she would like to call this kind of thinking. Remember to try to visualize this through pictures or write down what you are saying on a white board.

2. Begin educating the individual on the types of cognitive distortions. Get a treatment program manual, handbook, or worksheet (*Twisted Thinking Patterns, 2007-2015*) to explain each of the distorted thinking patterns. As you go through the list of cognitive distortions, definitions, and examples, ask the individual to put a check next to kind of distorted thinking he or she may engage in. It may be helpful to also tell them what kinds of distorted thinking patterns you engage in or if there are other family members in the room, they can share what they do.

3. For homework, have the individual complete a thought chart or diary (*Thought Chart, 2007-2015; Indentify the Distortion, 2007-2015*) where they record situations where they engage in negative thinking and have them identify the type of cognitive distortion they used.

4. When they return, review with them their homework and how often they engaged in the distorted thinking pattern.

5. Begin to review ways to challenge their cognitive distortions (*Ten Ways To Untwist Your Thinking, 2007-2015*). This may take several sessions. Once they begin to indentify one or more helpful ways to challenge their thinking patterns, then have them start challenging their thoughts at home with the use of another thought chart or diary (*Thought Chart, 2007-2015; Rational Response , 2007-2015*).

PHYSICAL SELF-REGULATION

Thermometer technique

The next step in teaching self-regulation strategies is to have the individual identify how they look and feel when they are happy, stressed, and angry. Professionals have created stress, pain, and anger thermometer strategies for years to assist with teaching self-regulation. Any type of thermometer or measuring tool can be helpful in working with an individual with ASD. Associating a thermometer or a different type of measuring tool with certain feelings can be helpful in teaching flexibility of emotions and thoughts.

To begin, we need to teach individuals with ASD the importance of recognizing when they are happy, stressed, or mad. We do this by giving them a blank thermometer (or other measuring tool) and teaching them to monitor their bodies like a thermometer ("1" means you are cold/happy, "5" means you are warm/stressed, "10" means you are hot/mad). Once they are able to understand these emotions and monitor how and when they feel a certain way, we can then teach them self-regulation strategies to stay calm.

Several sample worksheets, both for younger children as well as teens, are included in this chapter. First, have the student discuss what it means to be happy, stressed, and mad. It's helpful to have several students participate in the discussion as that will help the individual with ASD realize there are several different things that may happen to your body when are happy (e.g., smile, feel good), stressed (heart beats faster, start to frown), or mad (e.g., clinched fists, red face, screams). Have the individual with ASD write down all the ways he or she may express each emotion during different situations on the left side of the thermometer. For younger children, there are pictures of the three emotions on the worksheet. For older children, they may have more fun drawing what it looks like to feel that way.

Next, have the individual discuss what types of situations make them feel happy, stressed, or mad. Have them write down several situations that make them feel each emotion on the right side of the worksheet. Try to make this activity as visual as possible. Incorporate many of the social communication strategies discussed earlier, such as role playing, video monitoring, and social stories to help the individual understand each emotion and what happens to their body when they feel that emotion.

Once you are certain the individual with ASD understands the concepts of happy, stressed, and mad, it is time to teach self-regulation strategies. The basic self-regulation strategies include diaphragmatic breathing (or belly breathing), positive imagery, and progressive muscle relaxation.

Diaphragmatic breathing

Diaphragmatic breathing or belly breathing is a slow, deep breathing pattern that uses the diaphragm muscle rather than the chest muscles to expand and deflate the lungs. When we are first born, we breathe from our diaphragm. As we get older, we use a more shallow and rapid breathing pattern. Breathing from the diaphragm can help relieve headaches, stomachaches, anxiety, depression, and muscle tensions.

When we breathe, we inhale fresh oxygen and exhale carbon dioxide. Air enters our mouth or nose and travels down through our trachea or wind pipe into the tiny air sacs or alveoli, which are scattered throughout our lungs. The alveoli then pass oxygen into the blood and the blood passes carbon dioxide back into the alveoli. The new oxygenated blood then travels to the heart to be pumped throughout our bodies. The carbon dioxide is then exhaled when we breathe out. Our diaphragm is the muscle we use to breathe. The lungs actually don't have any muscles. The diaphragm is a large, flat muscle that separates the chest cavity from the abdominal cavity and stretches from one side of our rib cage to the other. As we breathe, the diaphragm muscle contracts and flattens downward making room for the lungs to fill up with air. The diaphragm pushes our abdominal organs down, which results in our bellies expanding, sort of like a balloon. When we exhale through our mouth, the diaphragm relaxes and returns to its original position. As a result, the muscles in our body become more relaxed.

Interestingly, most people breathe using short shallow breaths, mostly from their chest. This type of breathing usually increases during times of stress, anger, or pain, which causes some people then to have difficulty breathing. This is the opposite of diaphragmatic breathing, which promotes more oxygen exchange as more airs gets to the bottom of the lungs where most of the alveoli are located.

To practice diaphragmatic breathing, the individual with ASD should find a quiet, comfortable place to lie down or sit in a relaxed position. Have them close their eyes and begin to breathe in through their nose for 3 seconds. Their shoulders should be relaxed and still. As they breathe in, they should focus on their belly expanding, like a balloon. Then they should exhale out of their mouth for 5 seconds and their belly should deflate. When they practice, you can make it fun by having them blow bubbles, play a harmonica, or put a book on their belly and watch the book go up and down.

Positive imagery

Positive imagery is a stress reduction technique that helps the individual with ASD focus on the positive aspects of a certain environment, imaginary or real. Once an individual has learned how to do diaphragmatic breathing, you can teach them how to do positive imagery. The goal is to have the individual relax through diaphragmatic breathing, then have the individual imagine a place with all of their senses. They are to imagine what they would see, hear, touch, taste, and smell. By engaging all the senses, it allows the individual to block out everything else around them, including any negative thoughts. Because individuals with ASD are typically visual, this can be quite useful. If I am working with someone with ASD who is younger, lower functioning, or just having a difficult time redirecting to something positive, I will add visual pictures of a place that I know they like while we use diaphragmatic breathing. Seeing the actual pictures may also help redirect their thoughts.

Progressive muscle relaxation

Progressive muscle relaxation (PMR) is another self-regulation technique that focuses on relaxing specific groups of muscles. The individual is instructed to focus on a certain muscle and to first tighten the muscle and notice how the muscle feels different when it is tight and tense, and then relax the muscle, so they compare the difference in how that muscle feels when it is loose and relaxed. It works best if someone reads a PMR script or plays an audio recording. Typically, libraries have recordings available.

It is important to provide the included handouts (or similar handouts) to the parents and individuals with ASD on each of these self-regulation techniques. It is extremely important to practice and model all of these strategies with both the individual and their caregiver, as they will need to practice these strategies at home as much as possible. Once they have learned some effective coping strategies to stay calm and regulate their bodies, then have them complete the calming thermometer worksheet. Have them write/draw again how it feels to be happy, stressed, and mad on the left side of the thermometer. On the right side, have the students write down the strategies that help them relax and/or calm down.

Worksheet

I am Feeling

Directions: Circle the emotion, then complete the sentence below.

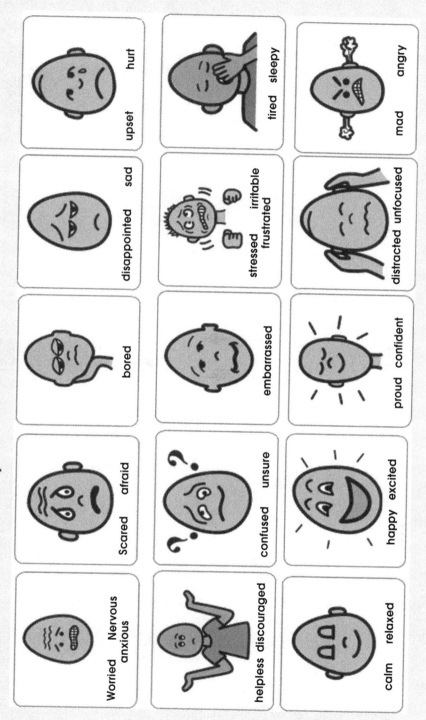

upset hurt	disappointed sad	bored	Scared afraid	Worried Nervous anxious
tired sleepy	stressed irritable frustrated	embarrassed	confused unsure	helpless discouraged
mad angry	distracted unfocused	proud confident	happy excited	calm relaxed

I am feeling _____ because _____ .

Made with Boardmaker® and the Picture Communication Symbols © 1981-2010 Mayer-Johnson LLC - 2100 Wharton St. Suite 400. Pittsburgh, PA 15203 U.S.A. Phone (800)588-4548. www.mayer-johson.com

Worksheet
Learning "I" Statements

Directions: "I" statements tell how I am feeling and state the problem. Remember to not say "you" in an "I" statement. Only talk about the situation and not the person. **Example: I feel angry when I am late to class. I wish I had more time to get to class.**

I feel _____ when _____

_____.

I wish _____

_____.

I feel _____ when _____

_____.

I wish _____

_____.

I feel _____ when _____

_____.

I wish _____

_____.

I feel _____ when _____

_____.

I wish _____

Ten Forms of Twisted Thinking

1. **All or Nothing Thinking.** You see things in black or white categories. There is no flexibility in your thinking. If a situation falls short of perfect, you see it as a total failure. *When a girl gets one question wrong on a test, she thinks, "I failed the test, there's no point in studying for anything else."*

2. **Overgeneralization.** You see a single negative event, criticism from a teacher, as a never-ending pattern of defeat by using words such as 'always' or 'never' when you think about it. *You ask a girl out and she says 'no.' You think, "No one likes me."*

3. **Mental Filter.** You pick out a single negative detail and dwell on it exclusively, so that your vision of all reality becomes darkened, like the drop of ink that discolors a glass of water. *Your parent tells you that you did a great job cleaning your room, but that you forgot to put* one *toy away. You ignore the compliment and only focus on what you did wrong.*

4. **Discounting the Positive.** You reject positive experiences by insisting they 'don't count'. *If you do a good job, you may tell yourself that it was not good enough or that anyone could have done as well.* Discounting the positive takes the joy out of life and makes you feel inadequate and unrewarded.

5. **Jumping to Conclusions.** You interpret things negatively when there are no facts to support your conclusion.

   Mind Reading. Without checking it out, you randomly conclude that someone is reacting negatively to you. *"I think the boy next to me gave me a dirty look; he must hate me."*

   Fortune Telling. You predict things will turn out badly. *Before a test you may tell yourself, 'I'm really going to blow it. What if I flunk?"* If you're depressed, you may tell yourself, "I'll never get better."*

6. **Magnification and Minimization.** You exaggerate the importance of your problems and shortcomings. Or you minimize the importance of your desirable qualities. *"I am scared I will get in a car accident since I have never driven before, so I am not going to learn how to drive."*

7. **Emotional Reasoning.** You think that your negative emotions are the way things really are. *"I feel guilty. I must be a rotten person."* Or *"I feel angry. This proves someone is treating me wrong".* Or *"I feel hopeless. I must really be hopeless."*

8. **'Should' Statements.** You tell yourself that things *should* be the way you hoped or expected them to be. *After playing a difficult song on a piano, a very good pianist told herself, "I shouldn't have made so many mistakes'."* This made her feel so bad that she quit practicing for several days. 'Must', 'ought to's, and 'have to's are similar offenders.

   'Should' statements that are directed against yourself lead to guilt and frustration. 'Should' statements that are directed against other people or the world lead to anger and frustration: *'He shouldn't be so stubborn and argumentative.'*

   Many people try to motivate themselves with 'should's and 'shouldn'ts' as if they have to be punished before they could be expected to do anything. *"I shouldn't eat that cookie."* This usually doesn't work, because all these 'shoulds' and 'musts' make you feel rebellious and you get the urge to do just the opposite.

9. **Labeling.** Labeling is an extreme form of all-or-nothing thinking. *Instead of saying 'I made a mistake', you attach a negative label to yourself: "I'm a loser." You might also label yourself "a fool" or "a failure" or "a jerk."* These labels are useless thoughts that lead to anger, anxiety, frustration, and low self-esteem.

   You may also label others. *When someone does something that makes you mad, you may tell yourself: 'He's a dummy.'* Then you feel like the problem is in that person's 'character' instead of in what they're thinking or their behavior. You see them as totally bad. This makes you feel mean and hopeless about improving things and leaves little room for good communication.

10. **Personalization and Blame.** Personalization occurs when you hold yourself personally responsible for an event that isn't entirely under your control. *A girl's parents get into heated arguments, and she thinks, 'If only I was a better daughter, my parents wouldn't fight.'* Personalization leads to guilt, shame, and feelings of inadequacy.

    Some people do the opposite. They blame other people or their situation for their problems, and they overlook ways that they might be contributing to the problem: *A student gets in trouble for hitting another kid. He says 'He made me do it'.* Blame usually doesn't work very well because other people don't like being blamed and they will toss the blame right back in your lap. It's like the game of hot potato—no one wants to get stuck with it.

Adapted from David D. Burns *The Feeling Good Handbook* (1999).

Ten Ways to Untwist Your Thinking

1. **Identify the Distortion.** Write down your negative thoughts, so you can see which of the ten forms of twisted thinking you're caught up in. This will make it easier to think about the problem in a more positive and realistic way.

2. **Examine the Evidence.** Instead of thinking your negative thought is true, examine the actual evidence for it. *For example, if you feel that you never do anything right, make a list of several things you have done right.*

3. **The Double Standard Method.** Instead of putting yourself down in a harsh way, talk to yourself in a kind way, like the way you would talk to a friend.

4. **The Experimental Technique.** Do an experiment to test if your negative thought is correct. *For example, if you think there are monsters under your bed, take a look!*

5. **Thinking in Gray.** Instead of thinking about your problems in all-or-nothing extremes, grade things on a scale of 0 to 100. When things don't work out as well as you hoped, think about the experience as a small success rather than a complete failure. See what lessons you can learn.

6. **The Survey Method.** Ask people questions to find out if your thoughts and attitudes are realistic. *For example, if you feel like its weird to be scared or nervous when meeting new people, you can ask your parents or friends if they have ever felt that way.*

7. **Define Words.** When you label yourself "a loser" or "a fool", ask, *"What is the definition of a fool?"* You will feel better when you see that there is no such thing as a 'fool' or a 'loser'.

8. **The Substitution Method.** Simply substitute words that are less harsh or emotional; this method is helpful for 'should' statements. Instead of telling yourself, '*I shouldn't have made that mistake*', you can say '*It would be better if I hadn't made that mistake.*'

9. **Finding the Cause.** Instead of automatically assuming that you are "bad" and blaming yourself entirely for a problem, think about the many things that may have contributed to it. Focus on solving the problem instead of using up all your energy blaming yourself and feeling guilty.

10. **Plus-Minus List.** List the pluses and minuses of a feeling (*like getting angry when your brother or sister take your toy*), or a negative thought (like "*No matter how hard I try, I always mess up*"). You can also use the Plus-Minus list to change a self-defeating belief such as, "*I must always try to be perfect.*"

Adapted from David D. Burns, The Feeling Good Handbook, 1999

Thought Chart: Identify the Distortion

Directions: Complete the information below to identify what type of cognitive distortion was used in the situation that occurred. An example has been provided to help you.

Situation	Emotion	Automatic Thought	Cognitive Distortion
Describe situation that occurred.	**Label the feeling and rank how strong it is on a scale from 1 to 10.**	**Write down the thought you had.**	**Identify the cognitive distortion or twisted thinking pattern.**
Mom tells me to get off video game	Frustrated - 8	She never lets me finish a game.	Over-generalization

Thought Chart: Rational Response

Directions: Complete the information below to change the cognitive distortion into a rational response. An example has been provided to help you.

Situation	Emotion	Automatic Thought	Cognitive Distortion	Rational Response	Outcome
Describe situation that occurred.	Label the feeling and rank how strong it is on a scale from 1 to 10.	Write down the thought you had.	Identify the cognitive distortion or twisted thinking pattern.	Identify a way to untwist your thinking and then write rational thought.	Label your feeling and rank how strong it is on a scale from 1 to 10.
Mom tells me to get off video game	Frustrated - 8	She never lets me finish a game.	Over-generalization	Examined the evidence – she did let me finish the game last Monday. I'll ask her when I can finish the game.	Frustrated – 3

Feelings Thermometer

Directions: Write, draw, or describe what you may look like or do when at different levels on the thermometer.

What I may look like or do:

What makes me feel this way:

Scream, red face, hit, run to room, clinch teeth, scrunch up face

Heart beats faster, start to frown, get hot, my hands move back and forth

Smile, show teeth, body feels light, laugh

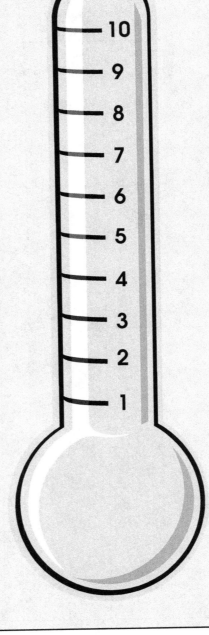

MAD

Being told "No!"

Not being able to play the computer

My brother/sister bugging me

STRESSED

Homework

Getting teased

Something changes that I was not expecting

HAPPY

My dog

Playing with friends

Playing the computer

Ice Cream

Feelings Thermometer

Directions: Write, draw, or describe what you may look like or do when at different levels on the thermometer. For example, at a 1, you may feel happy, but at a 10, you may be extremely mad.

What I may look like or do:

What makes me feel this way:

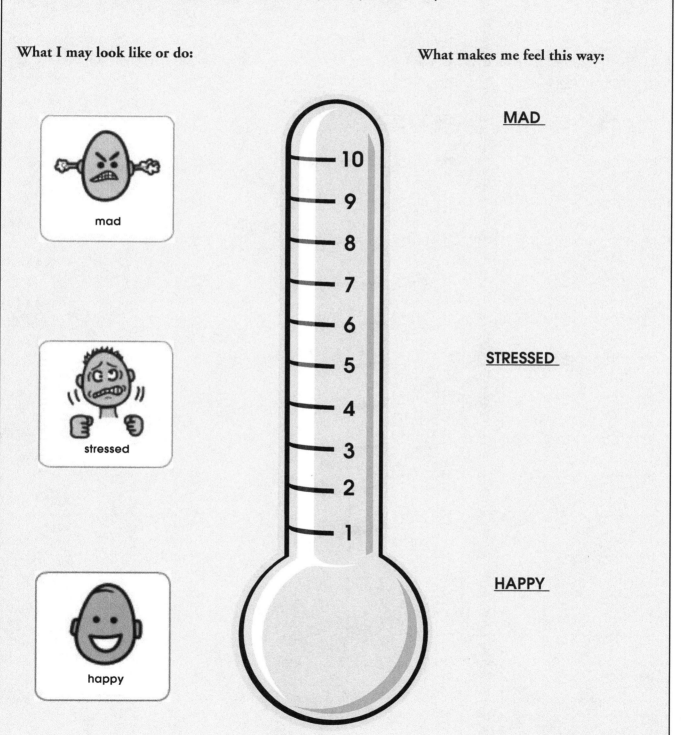

Feelings Thermometer

Directions: Write, draw, or describe what you may look like or do when at different levels on the thermometer. For example, at a 1, you may feel happy, but at a 10, you may be extremely mad.

What I may look like or do: **What makes me feel this way:**

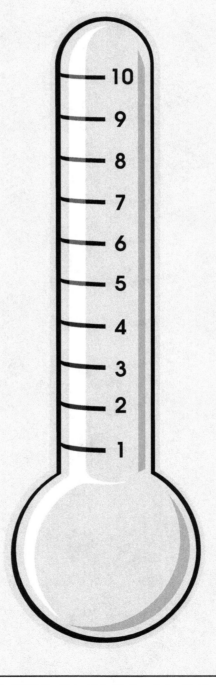

Calming Thermometer

Directions: To the left of the thermometer, write, draw, or describe what you may look like or do when at different levels on the thermometer. For example, at a 1, you may feel happy, but at a 10, you may feel extremely mad. To the right of the thermometer, write, draw, or describe ways to calm down.

What I may look like or do:

How I calm down:

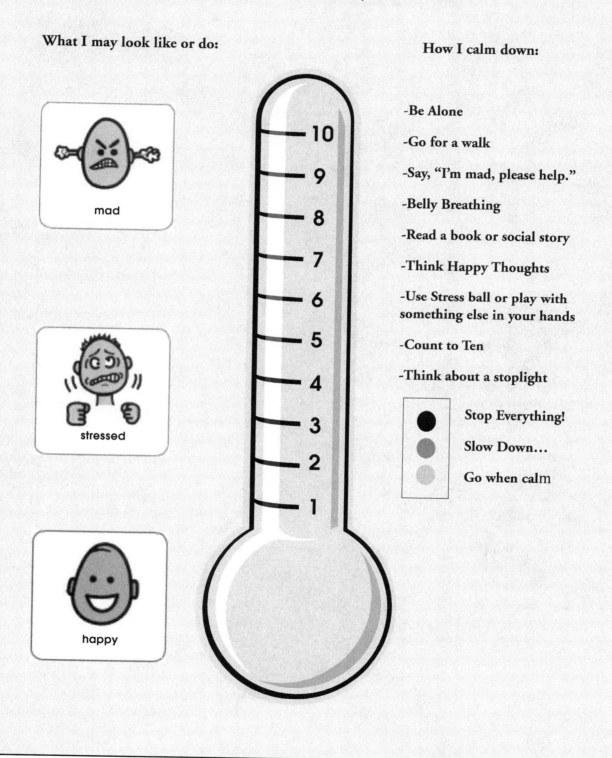

mad

stressed

happy

- Be Alone

- Go for a walk

- Say, "I'm mad, please help."

- Belly Breathing

- Read a book or social story

- Think Happy Thoughts

- Use Stress ball or play with something else in your hands

- Count to Ten

- Think about a stoplight

Stop Everything!

Slow Down…

Go when calm

Calming Thermometer

Directions: Write, draw, or describe what makes you feel each emotion that you labeled on the thermometer.

What I may look like or do: **How I calm down:**

Calming Thermometer

Directions: Write, draw, or describe what makes you feel each emotion that you labeled on the thermometer.

What I may look like or do:

How I calm down:

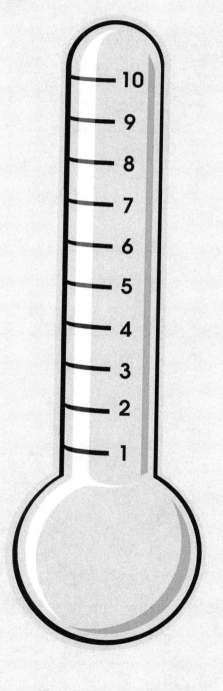

What's My Temperature?

Directions: Read each statement and complete the sentence based on how you would feel in that situation. Next to each statement, mark how it would make you feel on a scale from 1 to 10 on the thermometer. For example, at a 1, you may feel happy, but at a 10, you may feel extremely mad.

1. If my brother or sister took my favorite game from me, I would feel…

_____

_____

_____

2. If I had to do more homework than I had planned, I would feel…

_____

_____

_____

3. If I could play my favorite game with a friend, I would feel…

_____

_____

_____

4. If my mom or dad told me that I did a good job, I would feel. . .

_____

_____

_____

5. If my teacher changed my schedule in class without telling me, I would feel. . .

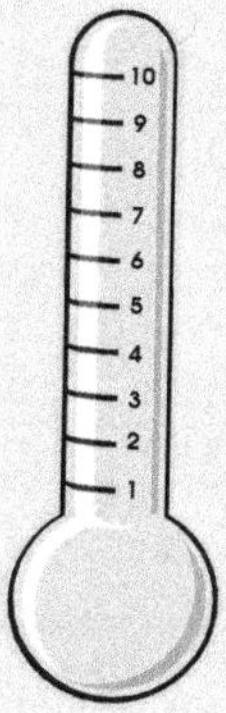

_____

_____

_____

_____

6. If I practiced at a game and got better at it, I would feel. . .

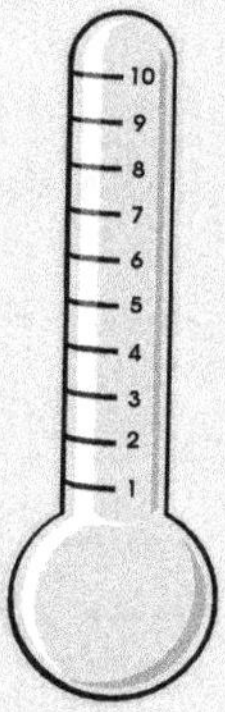

_____

_____

_____

_____

7. If my parents told me that I could not eat my favorite snack, I would feel. . .

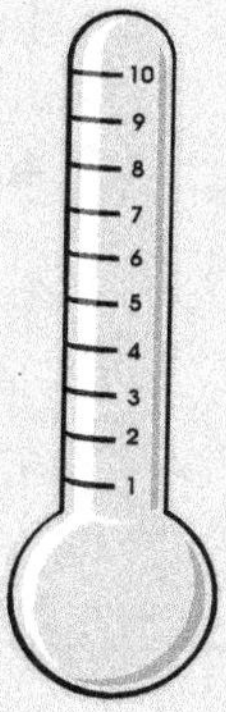

_____

_____

_____

_____

8. If I thought that my friend cheated on a game, I would feel...

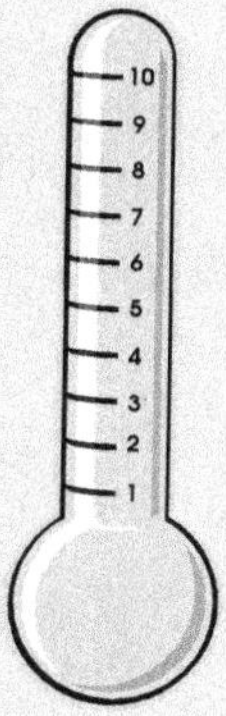

_____

_____

_____

_____

9. If my parents gave me a time out because of something I did, I would feel. . .

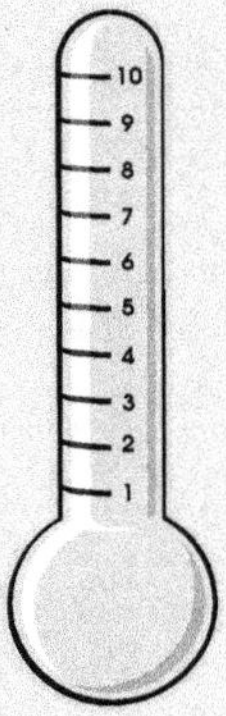

_____

_____

_____

_____

10. Think of something that would score a 10 on the thermometer, and write it here:

_____

_____

_____

_____

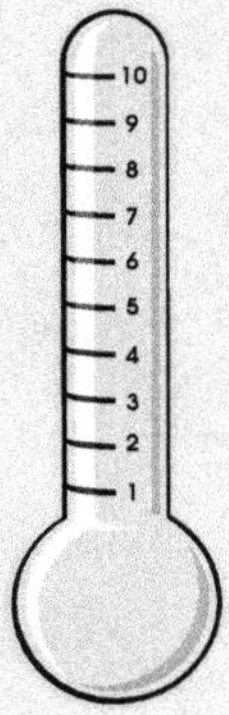

11. Think of something that would score a 5 on the thermometer, and write it here:

_____

_____

_____

_____

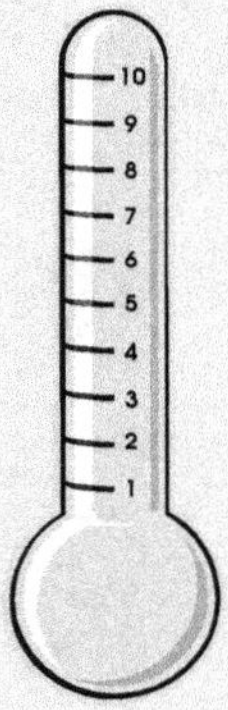

12. Think of something that would score a 1 on the thermometer, and write it here:

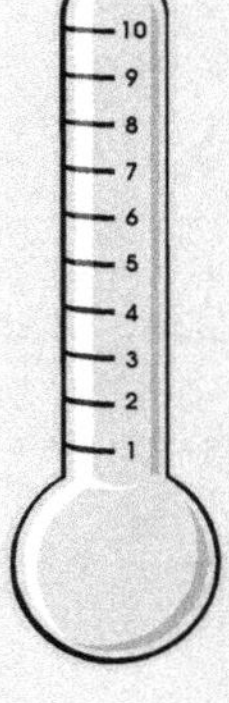

_____

_____

_____

_____

Diaphragmatic Breathing "BELLY BREATHING"

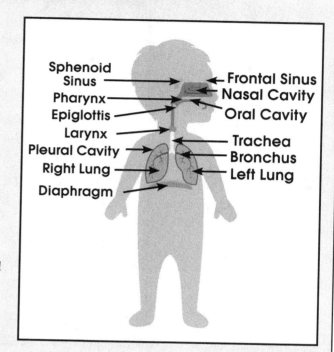

DIAPHRAGMATIC BREATHING HELPS YOU CALM DOWN BY:

- calming the nervous system
- slowing you heart rate
- releasing muscle tension
- lowering your blood pressure
- decreasing sweating

It is a great technique to use when you are nervous, stressed out, angry, or upset in any way!

HOW TO "BELLY BREATHE"

- Close your eyes
- Place your hand on your stomach
- Take a deep breath in through your nose for 3 seconds, and feel your stomach go up, almost like a balloon. Be careful to not let your shoulders go up, just expand your stomach.
- Breathe out through your mouth for 5 seconds
- Repeat until you feel calm and relaxed!

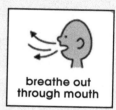

YOU CAN BELLY BREATHE AT ANY TIME AND ANYWHERE!

In some situations, it might feel a little awkward to close your eyes and hold your stomach, and that is why you have to practice and get really good at diaphragmatic breathing at home. If you practice, you will be able to "belly breathe" without anyone noticing. You can do it in school, with friends or at home, and all anybody will notice is your calm behavior.

Made with Boardmaker® and the Picture Communication Symbols © 1981-2010 Mayer-Johnson LLC - 2100 Wharton St. Suite 400. Pittsburgh, PA 15203 U.S.A. Phone (800)588-4548. www.mayer-johson.com

Positive Imagery

IMAGERY SCRIPT

Lie or sit in a comfortable position. Feel your body against the floor or the chair. Allow your body to soften and just let yourself be. And now allow your awareness to move to your breathing. Be aware of the in-breath. . . aware of the out-breath. . . breathing in, feeling calm, breathing out, and feeling at peace.

Now I'd like you to see yourself in a very special place. . . It could be a real place – a place you may have actually been – a beautiful spot in nature or comfortable spot in your own home. Your special place may be an imaginary place – a place in fairy tales – indoors or outdoors – it doesn't really matter. Should more than one place come to mind, allow yourself to stay with one of them.

The only thing that matters is that it is a place in which you are completely comfortable and safe. . . you feel comfortable and safe. Appreciate this scene with all your senses. Hear the sounds – smell the aromas, feel the air as it caresses your skin – experience the ground securely under you – touch and feel the whole environment that you are in.

Notice the colors that surround you. What is the temperature? Is it warm? Is it cold? Are you alone or are you with another person or people. Notice the qualities of the place that make it safe and comfortable.

Look around you to see if there is anything else that would make this place more safe for you. . . perhaps something that you need to remove from the place or something you need to bring in. . . and then notice how your body feels in this place. . . and now take some time to enjoy this feeling of safety in this special place. . .

Now thank yourself for taking the time. . . perhaps promising yourself and reassuring yourself that you will visit this place or some other place on your own, whenever you need to.

When you're ready. . . at your own pace. . . let your breathing deepen. . . very gradually let the awareness of your body against the floor or the chair return. . . and when you are ready. . . gently open your eyes.

Progressive Muscle Relaxation

Directions: *Relaxation skills* may help you cope with stress, anger, illness, sleep problems, injury or pain. Relaxation exercises are designed to help you recognize and reduce body tension.

As you complete each exercise, think about each group of muscles. Notice the difference between the tight and relaxed muscles. If a feeling *of tightness continues in any group of muscles after you have repeated the exercise several times, focus again on relaxing that particular muscle group. Your whole body should feel loose and relaxed.*

Legs

Sit or lie down with your legs straight. Point your toes toward your head. Hold this position and feel the tightness in your calf muscles. Relax your muscles and let your entire leg go limp. Focus on making your calf as loose as you can. Repeat this exercise.

Lift and extend both legs until you can feel the tightness in your thigh muscles. Hold this position, feel the tightness of your thigh muscles. Relax until all of the tightness in your thigh muscles is gone. Repeat this exercise. Try to keep your feet and ankles relaxed while you are tightening your thighs.

Chest and Abdomen

Take a deep breath and fill your lungs with air. Hold the air in your lungs. Feel the tightness in your chest and abdominal muscles. Now release the air and relax. Breath normally. Notice how easily the air moves when you are relaxed. Repeat this exercise.

Relax for a few seconds, then tighten, the muscles in your abdomen. Hold this position feeling the tightness of the muscles. Release your abdominal muscles and relax, breathing normally again. Repeat this exercise.

Hands and Arms

Make your hand into a fist; close your fist tightly and hold it closed. Feel the tightness in the muscles of your hand and forearm. Now relax your hand. Let it go limp and wiggle your fingers. Feel the tightness leave your hand and fingers. The muscles in your hand and forearm should feel relaxed. Remember to hold the relaxed position longer than the tense position. Do this exercise two times on each hand.

Upper Arms

Keeping your hands relaxed and arms straight, raise your hands to shoulder height. Bend your arms at the elbows so that your hands rise up; tighten the muscles in your upper arms. Count to 5 and then lower your arms until your hands hang limply at your sides. Notice how relaxed your muscles feel as you count to 5 again. Make your arms as loose as you can. Repeat this exercise.

Shoulders

Raise your shoulders to your ears and notice the tightness in the muscles in your shoulders and neck. Hold this position and think about how your muscles feel. Relax and drop your shoulders to their normal position. Relax your shoulders even more, letting them drop toward the floor. Notice the difference between the feeling of tightness and the feeling of relaxation. Repeat this exercise.

Neck

Move your head forward until your chin touches your chest. Notice the tension in the front of your neck, but especially in the back of your neck. Gradually put your head back in an upright position. Now put your head back as far as it will go, as if you were going to touch your head to your back. Notice where it is tense. Gradually put your head back in an upright position. This is the least tense position. While still in the relaxed position, tilt your head to the right, as if you were going to touch your head to your right shoulder. Bring your head back to the relaxed position. Now tilt your head to the left shoulder. Bring your head back to the relaxed position. Notice the difference when those muscles are loose and relaxed. Repeat exercise.

Face

Next, wrinkle your nose. Hold the position for five seconds and relax your face. Now tighten the muscles around your mouth and cheeks by putting your face in a forced smile. Your lips should be hard against your face. Notice how those muscles feel tight and tense. Gradually relax your face. Repeat the exercise.

References

For your convenience, you may download a PDF version of the worksheets in this book from our dedicated website: go.pesi.com/key

Abrahams, B. S., & Geschwind, D. H. (2008). Advances in autism genetics: on the threshold of a new neurobiology. *Nature Reviews Genetics, 9*(5), 341-355.

Achenbach, T. M., & Rescorla, L. (2001). *ASEBA school-age forms & profiles.* Burlington: Aseba.

Alexander, A. L., Lee, J. E., Lazar, M., Boudos, R., DuBray, M. B., Oakes, T. R., ... & Lainhart, J. E. (2007). Diffusion tensor imaging of the corpus callosum in Autism. *Neuroimage, 34*(1), 61-73.

Amaral, D. G., Schumann, C. M., & Nordahl, C. W. (2008). Neuroanatomy of autism. *Trends in neurosciences, 31*(3), 137-145.

American Occupational Therapy Association. (2010). The scope of occupational therapy services for individuals with an autism spectrum disorder across the life course. *American Journal of Occupational Therapy, 64* (6_Supplement), S125-S136.

American Psychiatric Association. (1952). *Diagnostic and statistical manual of mental disorders* (1st ed.). Washington, DC: *American Psychiatric Association.*

American Psychiatric Association. (1968). *Diagnostic and statistical manual of mental disorders* (2nd ed.). Washington, DC: *American Psychiatric Association.*

American Psychiatric Association. (2000). *Diagnostic and statistical manual of mental disorders* (4th ed., text rev.). Arlington, VA: *American Psychiatric Publishing.*

Arndt, T. L., Stodgell, C. J., & Rodier, P. M. (2005). The teratology of autism. *International Journal of Developmental Neuroscience, 23*(2), 189-199.

Ayres, A. J. (1989). Sensory integration and praxis test (SIPT). *Los Angeles: Western Psychological Services.*

Bailey, A., Le Couteur, A., Gottseman, I., Bolton, P., Simonoff, E., Yuzda, E., Rutter, M. (1995). Autism as a strongly genetic disorder: evidence from a British twin study. *Psychological Medicine, 25*(1), 63-77.

Baio, J. (2012). Prevalence of Autism Spectrum Disorders: Autism and Developmental Disabilities Monitoring Network, 14 Sites, United States, 2008. Morbidity and Mortality Weekly Report. Surveillance Summaries. Volume 61, Number 3. *Centers for Disease Control and Prevention.*

Baron-Cohen, S., Allen, J., & Gillberg, C. (1992). Can autism be detected at 18 months? The needles, the haystack, and the CHAT. *British Journal of Psychiatry, 161*(6), 839-843.

Bayley, N. (2006). *Bayley scales of infant and toddler development: Bayley-III* (Vol. 7). G. Reuner (Ed.). Harcourt Assessment, Psych. Corporation.

Beck, A. T. (1967). *Depression: Clinical, experimental, and theoretical aspects*(Vol. 32). University of Pennsylvania Press.

Bedrosian, J. (1985). An approach to developing conversational competence. *School discourse problems,* 231-255.

Bellini, S., Peters, J. K., Benner, L., & Hopf, A. (2007). A meta-analysis of school-based social skills interventions for children with autism spectrum disorders. *Remedial and Special Education, 28*(3), 153-162.

Berenguer-Forner, C., Miranda-Casas, A., Pastor-Cerezuela, G., & Rosello-Miranda, R. (2015). [Comorbidity of autism spectrum disorder and attention deficit with hyperactivity. A review study]. *Revista de neurologia, 60,* S37-43.

Bieber, J. (1994). Learning disabilities and social skills with Richard LaVoie: Last one picked ... first one picked on. *Washington, DC: Public Broadcasting Service.*

Bishop, D. V. M. (2003). *The Children's Communication Checklist: CCC-2.* London: Harcourt Assessment.

Bowers, L., Husingh, R., & LoGiudice, C. (2008). Social Language Development Test Elementary (SLDTE). Pro-ED.

Boyle, C. A., Boulet, S., Schieve, L. A., Cohen, R. A., Blumberg, S. J., Yeargin-Allsopp, M., ... & Kogan, M. D. (2011). Trends in the prevalence of developmental disabilities in US children, 1997–2008. *Pediatrics,* peds-2010.

Brannigan, G., & Decker, S. (2003). *Bender visual-motor Gestalt test, (Bender Gestalt II).* Itasca, IL: Riverside Publishing.

Brandwein, A. B., Foxe, J. J., Butler, J. S., Russo, N. N., Altschuler, T. S., Gomes, H., & Molholm, S. (2012). The Development of Multisensory Integration in High-Functioning Autism: High-Density Electrical Mapping. and Psychophysical Measures Reveal Impairments in the Processing of Audiovisual Inputs. *Cerebral Cortex, 23*(6), 1329–1341.

Bricker, D., Squires, J., Mounts, L., Potter, L., Nickel, R., Twombly, E., & Farrell, J. (1999). Ages and stages questionnaires. *Baltimore, MD: Paul H. Brookes.*

Brownell, R. (Ed.). (2000). *Expressive one-word picture vocabulary test.* Academic Therapy Publications.

Bruininks, R. H. (2005). Bruininks-Oseretsky Test of Motor Proficiency, (BOT-2). *Minneapolis, MN: Pearson Assessment.*

Burns, D. D. (1999). *The feeling good handbook.* New York: Plume.

Catani, M., Jones, D. K., Daly, E., Embiricos, N., Deeley, Q., Pugliese, L., ... & Murphy, D. G. (2008). Altered cerebellar feedback projections in Asperger syndrome. *Neuroimage, 41*(4), 1184-1191.

Cappadocia, M. C., & Weiss, J. A. (2011). Review of social skills training groups for youth with Asperger syndrome and high functioning autism. *Research in Autism Spectrum Disorders, 5*(1), 70-78.

Carrow-Woolfolk, E. (1999). *CASL: Comprehensive Assessment of Spoken Language.* Circle Pines, MN: American Guidance Services.

Cohen, H., Amerine-Dickens, M., & Smith, T. (2006). Early intensive behavioral treatment: Replication of the UCLA model in a community setting. *Journal of Developmental & Behavioral Pediatrics, 27(2),* S145-S155.

Cohen, M. (1997). Children's Memory Scale (CMS). San Antonio, TX: *Psychological Corporation.*

Conners, C.K. (2008). Conners' Rating Scales – Revised: Manual. Tonawanda, NY: *Multi-Health Systems.*

Constantino, J.N., & Gruber, C. P. (2012). Social responsiveness scale, Second Edition. Los Angeles, CA: *Western Psychological Services.*

Courchesne, E., Carper, R., & Akshoomoff, N. (2003). Evidence of brain overgrowth in the first year of life in autism. *Jama, 290*(3), 337-344.

Courchesne, E., Mouton, P. R., Calhoun, M. E., Semendeferi, K., Ahrens-Barbeau, C., Hallet, M. J., ... & Pierce, K. (2011). Neuron number and size in prefrontal cortex of children with autism. *Jama, 306*(18), 2001-2010.

Courchesne, E., Pierce, K., Schumann, C. M., Redcay, E., Buckwalter, J. A., Kennedy, D. P., & Morgan, J. (2007). Mapping early brain development in autism. *Neuron, 56*(2), 399-413.

Croen, L. A., Najjar, D. V., Fireman, B., & Grether, J. K. (2007). Maternal and paternal age and risk of autism spectrum disorders. *Archives of pediatrics & adolescent medicine, 161*(4), 334-340.

Daily Behavioral Health. [Worksheet].(n.d.). N.p. (2007-2015).

Dajani, D. R. and Uddin, L. Q. (2015). Local brain connectivity across development in autism spectrum disorder: A cross-sectional investigation. *Autism Research.*

Dapretto, M., Davies, M. S., Pfeifer, J. H., Scott, A. A., Sigman, M., Bookheimer, S. Y., & Iacoboni, M. (2006). Understanding emotions in others: mirror neuron dysfunction in children with autism spectrum disorders. *Nature neuroscience, 9*(1), 28-30.

Dawson, G., Rogers, S., Munson, J., Smith, M., Winter, J., Greenson, J., ... & Varley, J. (2010). Randomized, controlled trial of an intervention for toddlers with autism: the Early Start Denver Model. *Pediatrics, 125*(1), e17-e23.

Delis, D. C., Kaplan, E., & Kramer, J. H. (2001). *Delis-Kaplan Executive Function System (D-KEFS).* San Antonio: TX: Psychological Corporation.

Dietz, C., Swinkels, S., van Daalen, E., van Engeland, H., & Buitelaar, J. K. (2006). Screening for autistic spectrum disorder in children aged 14–15 months. II: population screening with the Early Screening of Autistic Traits Questionnaire (ESAT). Design and general findings. *Journal of autism and developmental disorders, 36*(6), 713-722.

Dölen, G., Osterweil, E., Rao, B. S., Smith, G. B., Auerbach, B. D., Chattarji, S., & Bear, M. F. (2007). Correction of fragile X syndrome in mice. *Neuron, 56*(6), 955-962.

DSM-5 American Psychiatric Association. (2013). Diagnostic and statistical manual of mental disorders (5th ed.). Arlington, VA: *American Psychiatric Publishing.*

Duchan, E., & Patel, D. R. (2012). Epidemiology of autism spectrum disorders. *Pediatric Clinics of North America, 59*(1), 27-43.

Dunn, W. (1999). Short Sensory Profile. *San Antonio, TX: Psychological Corporation.*

Dunn, D. M., & Dunn, L. (2007). *Peabody Picture Vocabulary Test: Manual.*. Pearson.

Dykes, M. K., & Erin, J. N. (1999). *A Developmental Assessment for Students with Severe Disabilities—.*

Eden Autism Services (1990). *Eden Autism Assessment and Curriculum Series.* Eden Institute, Inc.

Edwards, S., Fletcher P., Garman, M., Highes, A., Letts, C., & Sinka, I. (1999). *Reynell Developmental Language Scales –III.* Windsor, UK: NFER-Nelson.

Ehlers, S., Gillberg, C., & Wing, L. (1999). A screening questionnaire for Asperger syndrome and other high-functioning autism spectrum disorders in school age children. *Journal of autism and developmental disorders, 29*(2), 129-141.

Folio, M., and Fewell, R. (2000). *Peabody Developmental Motor Scales. Examiners Manual.* 2nd ed. Austin, TX.

Frey, H. P., Molholm, S., Lalor, E. C., Russo, N. N., & Foxe, J. J. (2013). Atypical cortical representation of peripheral visual space in children with an autism spectrum disorder. *European Journal of Neuroscience, 38*(1), 2125-2138.

Frith, U.T. (1991). *Autism and Asperger's Syndrome.* Cambridge; Cambridge University Press, pp. 37–92.

Geschwind, D. H. (2009). Advances in autism. *Annual review of medicine, 60, 367.*

Geschwind, D. H. (2011). Genetics of Autism Spectrum Disorders. *Trends in Cognitive Sciences, 15*(9), 409–416.

Gilliam, J. E. (2013). *Gilliam Autism Rating Scale-Third Edition.* Austin, TX: *Pro-Ed.*

Gioia, G. A., Isquith, P. K., Guy, S. C., & Kenworthy, L. (2000). *Behavior rating inventory of executive function.* Odessa, FL: *Psychological Assessment Resources.*

Girolametto, L. (1997). Development of a parent report measure for profiling the conversational skills of preschool children. *American Journal of Speech-Language Pathology, 6*(4), 25-33.

Glascoe FP. (2010, July). Parents' Evaluation of Developmental Status (PEDS). Nolensville, TN: *PEDSTest.com*, LLC. Retrieved August 31, 2015 from http://www.pedstest.com/AboutOurTools/LearnAboutPEDSDM.aspx

Golden, C. J., Freshwater, S. M., & Golden, Z. (2004*). Stroop Color and Word Test: Children's Version.* Wood Dale, IL: Stoelting.

Goldman, H. (2002). *Augmentative Communication Assessment Profile.* London: Speechmark.

Goldstein, H. (2002). Communication intervention for children with autism: A review of treatment efficacy. *Journal of Autism and Developmental Disorders, 32(5), 373-396.*

Goldstein, S., Naglieri, J. A., & Ozonoff, S. (Eds.). (2008). *Assessment of autism spectrum disorders.* Guilford Press.

Gray, C. (1994). *Comic strip conversations: Illustrated interactions that teach conversation skills to students with autism and related disorders.* Future Horizons.

Gray, C. (2010). *The new social story book.* Future Horizons.

Greenspan, S. I., & Wieder, S. (1997). An integrated developmental approach to interventions for young children with severe difficulties in relating and communicating. *Zero to Three, 17,* 5-18.

Gutstein, S. E., Burgess, A. F., & Montfort, K. (2007). Evaluation of the relationship development intervention program. *Autism, 11*(5), 397-411.

Handen, B. L., Johnson, C. R., & Lubetsky, M. (2000). Efficacy of methylphenidate among children with autism and symptoms of attention-deficit hyperactivity disorder. *Journal of autism and developmental disorders, 30*(3), 245-255.

Hardan, A. Y., Gengoux, G. W., Berquist, K. L., Libove, R. A., Ardel, C. M., Phillips, J., ... & Minjarez, M. B. (2014). A randomized controlled trial of Pivotal Response Treatment Group for parents of children with autism. *Journal of Child Psychology and Psychiatry.*

Harrison, P., & Oakland, T. (2003). Adaptive Behavior Assessment System; (ABAS-II). *San Antonio, TX: The Psychological Corporation.*

Hazlett, H. C., Poe, M., Gerig, G., Smith, R. G., Provenzale, J., Ross, A., ... & Piven, J. (2005). Magnetic resonance imaging and head circumference study of brain size in autism: birth through age 2 years. *Archives of general psychiatry,62*(12), 1366-1376.

Heaton, R. K., Chelune, G. J., Talley, J.L., Kay, G. G., & Curtis, G. (1993). Wisconsin Card Sorting Test (WCST) manual revised and expanded. Odessa, FL: *Psychological Assessment Resources.*

Henderson, S., & Sugden, D. (1992). *Movement Assessment Battery for Children: Manual.* London: *The Psychological Corporation.*

Hernandez, N., Metzger, A., Magne, R., Bonnet-Brilhault, F., Roux, S., Barthelemy, C. & Martineau, J. (2009) Exploration of core features of a human face by healthy and autistic adults analyzed by visual scanning. *Neuropsychologia, 47*(4), 1004-1012

Horner, R., Carr, E. G., Strain, P. S., Todd, A. W., & Reed, H. K. (2002). Problem behavior intervention for young child with autism: A research synthesis. *Journal of Autism and Developmental Disorders, 32(5),* 423.

Hourcade, Jack; Pilotte, Tami Everhart; West, Elizabeth; and Parette, Phil. (2004). A History of Augmentative and Alternative Communication for Individuals with Severe and Profound Disabilities. *Focus on Autism and Other Developmental Disabilities, 19*(4), 235-244.

Hresko, W., Reid, K., & Hamill, D. (1999). *TELD-3: Test of Early Language Development: Examiner's Manual.*. Austin, TX: Pro-ed.

Hutchins, T. L., & Prelock, P. A. (2006, February). Using social stories and comic strip conversations to promote socially valid outcomes for children with autism. In *Seminars in Speech and Language* (Vol. 27, No. 1, pp. 47-59).

IbaÑez, L. V., Stone, W. L., & Coonrod, E. E. (2014). Screening for autism in young children. *Handbook of Autism and Pervasive Developmental Disorders, Fourth Edition*.

Iacoboni, M., & Dapretto, M. (2006). The mirror neuron system and the consequences of its dysfunction. *Nature Reviews Neuroscience, 7*(12), 942-951.

Just, M. A., Cherkassky, V. L., Keller, T. A., Kana, R. K., & Minshew, N. J. (2007). Functional and anatomical cortical underconnectivity in autism: evidence from an FMRI study of an executive function task and corpus callosum morphometry. *Cerebral cortex, 17*(4), 951-961.

Johnson, C. P., & Myers, S. M. (2007). Identification and evaluation of children with autism spectrum disorders. *Pediatrics, 120*(5), 1183-1215.

Kana, R.K., Keller, T.A., Cherkassky, V.L., Minshew, N.J, & Just, M.A. (2006). Sentence comprehension in autism: Thinking in pictures with decreased functional connectivity. *Brain, 129(9),* 2484–2493

Kanner, L. (1943). *Autistic disturbances of affective contact* (pp. 217-250). publisher not identified.

Kaufmann, W. E. (2012, October). DSM-5: The new diagnostic criteria for autism spectrum disorders. In *Research Symposium-Autism Consortium, Boston, MA*.

Kendall, P.C., Choudhury, M., Hudson, J.L., & Webb, A. (2001). The C.A.T. project: *Cognitive behavioral treatment for anxious adolescents*. Ardmore, PA: Workbook publishing.

Kendall, P. C., & Hedtke, K. (2006). *Coping Cat workbook*. (2nd ed). Ardmore, PA: Workbook Publishing.

Kleiman, L. I. (2003). *Functional Communication Scale* – profile-revised. *Austin: Lingui Systems*.

Kliemann, D., Dziobek, I., Hatri, A., Steimke, R., & Heekeren, H. R. (2010). Atypical reflexive gaze patterns on emotional faces in autism spectrum disorders. *The Journal of Neuroscience, 30*(37), 12281-12287.

Koegel, R. L., & Kern Koegel, L. (2006). *Pivotal Response Treatments for Autism: Communication, Social, and Academic Development*. Brookes Publishing Company. Baltimore, MD.

Kogan, M. D., Blumberg, S. J., Schieve, L. A., Boyle, C. A., Perrin, J. M., Ghandour, R. M., ... & van Dyck, P. C. (2009). Prevalence of parent-reported diagnosis of autism spectrum disorder among children in the US, 2007. *Pediatrics, 124*(5), 1395-1403.

Kolevzon, A., Gross, R., & Reichenberg, A. (2007). Prenatal and perinatal risk factors for autism: a review and integration of findings. *Archives of pediatrics & adolescent medicine, 161*(4), 326-333.

Korkman, M., Kirk, U., & Kemp, S. (2007). *NEPSY – Second Edition*. (NEPSY II). San Antonio, TX: Harcourt Assessment.

Koshino, H., Carpenter, P.A., Minshew, N.J., Cherkassky, V., Keller, T.A., & Just, M.A. (2005). Functional connectivity in an fMRI working memory task in high functioning autism. *Neuroimage, 24(3),* 810–821.

Kutz, G. D. (2009, May). Seclusions and Restraints: Selected Cases of Death and Abuse at Public and Private Schools and Treatment Centers. Testimony Before the Committee on Education and Labor, House of Representatives. GAO-09-719T.*US Government Accountability Office*. Retrieved August 31, 2015 from http://www.gao.gov/new.items/d09719t.pdf.

Kwakye, L. D., Foss-Feig, J. H., Cascio, C. J., Stone, W. L., & Wallace, M. T. (2010). Altered Auditory and Multisensory Temporal Processing in Autism Spectrum Disorders. *Frontiers in Integrative Neuroscience, 4,* 129.

Lafayette Instruments (1999). *Purdue Pegboard Test – Revised Edition*. Lafayette, IN: Author.

Landa, R., Piven, J., Wzorek, M. M., Gayle, J. O., Chase, G. A., & Folstein, S. E. (1992). Social language use in parents of autistic individuals. *Psychological medicine*, *22*(01), 245-254.

Leark R. A., Greenberk, L.K., Kindschi, C. L., Dupuy, T, R., & Hughes, S. J. (2007). *Test of Variables of Attention: Professional Manual.* Los Alamitos, CA: The Tova Company.

Levy, S.E., Mandell, D.S., Schultz, R.T. (2009). Autism. *The Lancet*, 374:1627–1638

Lichtenstein, P., Carlström, E., Råstam, M., Gillberg, C., & Anckarsäter, H. (2010). The genetics of autism spectrum disorders and related neuropsychiatric disorders in childhood. *American Journal of Psychiatry*, *167*(11), 1357-1363.

Liu, Y., Cherkassky, V. L., Minshew, N. J., & Just, M. A. (2011). Autonomy of lower-level perception from global processing in autism: evidence from brain activation and functional connectivity. *Neuropsychologia*, *49*(7), 2105-2111.

Lord, C., Luyster, R., Gotham, K., & Guthrie, W. J. (2012). Autism diagnostic observation schedule—Toddler module. *Los Angeles: Western Psychological Services.*

Lord, C., & McGee, J. P. (2001). *Educating children with autism.* Washington, DC: National Academy Press.

Lord, C., Rutter, M., & Le Couteur, A. (1994). Autism Diagnostic Interview-Revised: a revised version of a diagnostic interview for caregivers of individuals with possible pervasive developmental disorders. *Journal of autism and developmental disorders*, *24*(5), 659-685.

Lovaas, O. I. (1987). Behavioral treatment and normal educational and intellectual functioning in young autistic children. *Journal of Consulting and Clinical Psychology, 55(1),* 3-9.

Marcus, R. N., Owen, R., Kamen, L., Manos, G., McQuade, R. D., Carson, W. H., & Aman, M. G. (2009). A placebo-controlled, fixed-dose study of aripiprazole in children and adolescents with irritability associated with autistic disorder.*Journal of the American Academy of Child & Adolescent Psychiatry*, *48*(11), 1110-1119.

Mariani, J., Coppola, G., Zhang, P., Abyzov, A., Provini, L., Tomasini, L., ... & Vaccarino, F. M. (2015). FOXG1-Dependent Dysregulation of GABA/Glutamate Neuron Differentiation in Autism Spectrum Disorders. *Cell, 162*(2), 375-390.

Marco, E. J., Hinkley, L. B. N., Hill, S. S., & Nagarajan, S. S. (2011). Sensory Processing in Autism: A Review of Neurophysiologic Findings. *Pediatric Research, 69,*(5 Pt 2), 48R–54R.

Matson, J. L., & Nebel-Schwalm, M. S. (2007). Comorbid psychopathology with autism spectrum disorder in children: An overview. *Research in developmental disabilities*, *28*(4), 341-352.

Mazzone, L., Ruta, L., & Reale, L. (2012). Psychiatric comorbidities in asperger syndrome and high functioning autism: diagnostic challenges. *Ann Gen Psychiatry*, *11*(1), 16.

McCarthy, C. F., McLean, L. K., Miller, J. F., Paul-Brown, D., Romski, M. A., Rourk, J. D., & Yoder, D. E. (1998). Communication supports checklist.*Baltimore: Paul H. Brookes.*

McCracken, J. T., McGough, J., Shah, B., Cronin, P., Hong, D., Aman, M. G., ... & McMahon, D. (2002). Risperidone in children with autism and serious behavioral problems. *New England Journal of Medicine*, *347*(5), 314-321.

McDougle, C. J., Holmes, J. P., Carlson, D. C., Pelton, G. H., Cohen, D. J., & Price, L. H. (1998). A double-blind, placebo-controlled study of risperidone in adults with autistic disorder and other pervasive developmental disorders.*Archives of General Psychiatry*, *55*(7), 633-641.

McDougle, C. J., Scahill, L., Aman, M. G., McCracken, J. T., Tierney, E., Davies, M., ... & Vitiello, B. (2005). Risperidone for the core symptom domains of autism: results from the study by the autism network of the research units on pediatric psychopharmacology. *American Journal of Psychiatry*, *162*(6):1142-1148.

McPheeters, M. L., Warren, Z., Sathe, N., Bruzek, J. L., Krishnaswami, S., Jerome, R. N., & Veenstra-VanderWeele, J. (2011). A systematic review of medical treatments for children with autism spectrum disorders. *Pediatrics,127*(5), e1312-e1321.

Mercer, (K). Examining DIR/Floortime ™ as a treatment for children with autism spectrum disorders: A review of research and theory. *Research on Social Work Practice*, 1049731515583062.

Mesibov, G., & Shea, V. (2009). The TEACCH Program in the Era of Evidence-Based Practice. *Journal of Autism and Developmental Disorders, 40*(5), 570-579.

Metz, B., Mulick, J.A., & Butter, E.M. (2005). A late-20th-century fad magnet. In J.W. Jacobson, R.M. Foxx, & J.A. Mulick (Eds.), *Controversial therapies for developmental disabilities: Fad, fashion, and science in professional practice* (237-263). Mahwah, NJ: Lawrence Erlbaum.

Miles, J. H. (2011). Autism spectrum disorders—a genetics review. *Genetics in Medicine, 13*(4), 278-294.

Minshew, N.J., Goldstein, G., & Siegel, D. (1997). Neuropsychologic functioning in autism: Profile of a complex information processing disorder. *Journal of the International Neuropsychological Society, 3(04)*, 303–316.

Mohammadzaheri, F., Koegel, L. K., Rezaei, M., & Bakhshi, E. (2015). A Randomized Clinical Trial Comparison Between Pivotal Response Treatment (PRT) and Adult-Driven Applied Behavior Analysis (ABA) Intervention on Disruptive Behaviors in Public School Children with Autism. *Journal of autism and developmental disorders*, 1-9.

Muhle, R., Trentacoste, S. V., & Rapin, I. (2004). The genetics of autism. *Pediatrics, 113*(5), e472-e486.

Myles, B. S., & Simpson, R. L. (1998). *Asperger Syndrome: A Guide for Educators and Parents*. Austin, TX: Pro-Ed. .

Newcomer, P.L., & Hammill, D.D. (2008). *Test of Language Development – Primary: Fourth Edition (TOLD – P:4)*. Austin, TX: Pro-Ed.

New York State Department of Health, Early Intervention Program. (1999*). Clinical practice guideline: The guideline technical report – autism/pervasive developmental disorders, assessment and intervention*. Albany, NC:.

Odom, S. L., Boyd, B. A., Hall, L. J., & Hume, K. (2010). Evaluation of comprehensive treatment models for individuals with autism spectrum disorders. *Journal of autism and developmental disorders, 40*(4), 425-436.

Odom, S. L., Brown, W. H., Frey, T., Karasu, N., Smith-Canter, L., & Strain, P. A. (2003). Evidence-based practices for young children with autism: Contributions from single-subject design research. *Focus on Autism and Other Developmental Disabilities, 18(3)*, 166-175.

Olson, L., & Marker, C. (2000). *Pine Grove School Teacher Inservice Manual*. Pine Grove School, South Carolina.

Ozonoff, S., & Cathcart, K. (1998). Effectiveness of a home program intervention for young children with autism. *Journal of Autism and Developmental Disorders, 28(1)*, 25–32.

Ozonoff, S., Young, G. S., Carter, A., Messinger, D., Yirmiya, N., Zwaigenbaum, L., ... & Stone, W. L. (2011). Recurrence risk for autism spectrum disorders: a Baby Siblings Research Consortium study. *Pediatrics, 128*(3), e488-e495.

Panerai, S., Ferrante, L., & Zingale, M. (2002). Benefits of the Treatment and Education of Autistic and Communication Handicapped Children (TEACCH) program as compared with a non specific approach. *Journal of intellectual disability research, 46*(4), 318-327.

Partington W.J. (2006). *The Assessment of Basic Language and Learning Skills -Revised*. Pleasant Hills, CA: Behavior Analysts, Inc.

Paul, R., Wilson, K. P., Goldstein, S., & Naglieri, J. A. (2009). Assessing speech, language, and communication in autism spectrum disorders. *Assessment of autism spectrum disorders*, 171-208.

Pelphrey, K. A., Shultz, S., Hudac, C. M. and Vander Wyk, B. C. (2011), Research Review: Constraining heterogeneity: the social brain and its development in autism spectrum disorder. *Journal of Child Psychology and Psychiatry, 52*(6), 631–644.

Persico, A.M., Bourgeron T. (2006). Searching for ways out of the autism maze: genetic, epigenetic and environmental clues. *Trends in Neuroscie*nce, *29*(7):349–58.

Phelps-Terasaki, D., & Phelps-Gunn, T. (1992). *The Test of Pragmatic Language – 2*. Austin, TX: Pro-Ed.

Piaget, J. (1952). *The Origins of Intelligence in Children*. New York: International Universities Press. (Vol. 8, No. 5, p. 18).

Posey, D. J., Puntney, J. I., Sasher, T. M., Kem, D. L., & McDougle, C. J. (2004). Guanfacine treatment of hyperactivity and inattention in pervasive developmental disorders: a retrospective analysis of 80 cases. *Journal of Child and Adolescent Psychopharmacology, 14*(2), 233-241.

Prutting, C. A., & Kirchner, D. M. (1983). Applied pragmatics. *Pragmatic assessment and intervention issues in language*, 29-64.

Quintana, H., Birmaher, B., Stedge, D., Lennon, S., Freed, J., Bridge, J., & Greenhill, L. (1995). Use of methylphenidate in the treatment of children with autistic disorder. *Journal of autism and developmental disorders, 25*(3), 283-294.

Reichow, B., & Volkmar, F. R. (2010). Social skills interventions for individuals with autism: Evaluation for evidence-based practices within a best evidence synthesis framework. *Journal of autism and developmental disorders, 40*(2), 149-166.

Reynolds, C. R., & Kamphaus, R. W. (2004). *BASC-2: Behavior assessment system for children*. John Wiley & Sons, Inc.

Rice, C. (2009). Prevalence of Autism Spectrum Disorders: Autism and Developmental Disabilities Monitoring Network, United States, 2006. Morbidity and Mortality Weekly Report. Surveillance Summaries. Volume 58, Number SS-10. *Centers for Disease Control and Prevention.*

Robins, D. L. (2008). Screening for autism spectrum disorders in primary care settings. *Autism, 12(5)*, 537-556.

Robins, D., Fein, D., & Barton, M. (2009). *Modified Checklist for Autism in Toddlers, Revised with Follow-up.* (M-CHAT-R/F) TM.

Rogers, S. J., Estes, A., Lord, C., Vismara, L., Winter, J., Fitzpatrick, A., . . . Dawson, G. (2012). Effects of a Brief Early Start Denver Model (ESDM)–Based Parent Intervention on Toddlers at Risk for Autism Spectrum Disorders: A Randomized Controlled Trial. *Journal of the American Academy of Child and Adolescent Psychiatry, 51*(10), 1052–1065.

Rogers, S. J., & Lewis, H. (1989). An effective day treatment model for young children with pervasive developmental disorders. *Journal of the American Academy of Child and Adolescent Psychiatry, 28(2)*, 207-214.

Roid, G. H. (2003). *Stanford-Binet Intelligence Scales, Fifth Edition.* Itasca, IL: Riverside.

Russo, N., Foxe, J. J., Brandwein, A. B., Altschuler, T., Gomes, H. and Molholm, S. (2010), Multisensory processing in children with autism: high-density electrical mapping of auditory–somatosensory integration. *Autism Research, 3*(5), 253–267.

Russo, N., Nicol, T., Trommer, B., Zecker, S., & Kraus, N. (2009). Brainstem transcription of speech is disrupted in children with autism spectrum disorders.*Developmental science, 12*(4), 557-567.

Rutter, M. (2000). Genetic studies of autism: from the 1970s into the millennium. *Journal of Abnormal Child Psychology, 28*(1), 3-14.

Rutter, M., Bailey, A., & Lord, C. (2003). *The social communication questionnaire: Manual.* Western Psychological Services.

Rutter, M., DiLavore, P. C., Risi, S., Gotham, K., & Bishop, S. L. (2012). *Autism diagnostic observation schedule: ADOS-2.* Los Angeles, CA: Western Psychological Services.

Sallows, G. O., & Graupner, T. D. (2005). Intensive behavioral treatment for children with autism: four-year outcome and predictors. *American Journal on Mental Retardation, 110* (6), 417-438.

Sandford, J. A., & Turner, A. . (2002). *Integrated visual and auditory continuous performance test manual.* Richmond, VA: BrainTrain.

Scherer, M. J. (1997). *Matching Assistive Technology & Child: A Process and Series of Assessments for Selecting and Evaluating Technologies Used by Infants and Young Children.* Institute for Matching Person & Technology.

Schmitz, C., & Rezaie, P. (2008). The neuropathology of autism: where do we stand?. *Neuropathology and applied neurobiology, 34*(1), 4-11.

Schopler, E. & Reichler, R. J. (1971). Parents as Co-therapists in the Treatment of Psychotic Children. *Journal of Autism and Childhood Schizophrenia* 1 (1), 87–102.

Schrank, Fredrick A., Nancy Mather, and Kevin S. McGrew. "Woodcock-Johnson IV Tests of Achievement." *Riverside: Rolling Meadows*, IL, USA(2014a).

Schrank, Fredrick A., Nancy Mather, and Kevin S. McGrew. "Woodcock-Johnson IV Tests of Cognitive Abilities." *Riverside: Rolling Meadows*, IL, USA(2014b).

Schumann, C. M., & Amaral, D. G. (2006). Stereological analysis of amygdala neuron number in autism. *The Journal of Neuroscience, 26*(29), 7674-7679.

Schumann, C. M., Hamstra, J., Goodlin-Jones, B. L., Lotspeich, L. J., Kwon, H., Buonocore, M. H., ... & Amaral, D. G. (2004). The amygdala is enlarged in children but not adolescents with autism; the hippocampus is enlarged at all ages. *The Journal of Neuroscience, 24*(28), 6392-6401.

Semel, E., Wiig, E. H., & Secord, W. (2004). *Clinical Evaluation of Language Fundamentals – Preschool, Second Edition (CELF-Preschool 2).* San Antonio, TX: Harcourt Assessment.

Sheslow, D., & Adams, W. (2003). *Wide Range Assessment of Memory and Learning,* (2nd ed.). San Antonio, TX: Harcourt Assessment.

Schriberg, L. D., Kwiatkowski, J., & Rasmussen, C. (1990). *The Prosody-Voice Screening Profile (PVSP): Scoring forms and training materials.*.Tucson, AZ: Communication Skill Builders.

Smith, I. M., Flanagan, H. E., Garon, N., & Bryson, S. E. (2015). Effectiveness of Community-Based Early Intervention Based on Pivotal Response Treatment. *Journal of autism and developmental disorders, 45*(6), 1858-1872.

Sparrow, S.S., Cicchetti, D.V., & Balla, D.A. (2005). *Vineland Adaptive Behavior Scales, Second Edition*. Circle Pines: MN: American Guidance Service.

Spitzer, R. L., Md, K. K., & Williams, J. B. (1980). Diagnostic and statistical manual of mental disorders. In *American Psychiatric Association*.

Squires, J., Twombly, E., Bricker, D., & Potter, L. (2009). *The ASQ-3™ User's Guide*. Baltimore, MD: Paul H. Brookes Publishing Co., Inc.

Sundberg, M. L. (2008) *Verbal behavior milestones assessment and placement program: The VB-MAPP*. Concord, CA: AVB Press.

Sussman, D., Leung, R. C., Vogan, V. M., Lee, W., Trelle, S., Lin, S., ... & Taylor, M. J. (2015). The autism puzzle: Diffuse but not pervasive neuroanatomical abnormalities in children with ASD. *NeuroImage: Clinical, 8,* 170-179.

Sutton, G. P., Barchard, K. A., Bello, D. T., Thaler, N. S., Ringdahl, E., Mayfield, J., & Allen, D. N. (2011). Beery-Buktenica Developmental Test of Visual-Motor Integration performance in children with traumatic brain injury and attention-deficit/hyperactivity disorder. *Psychological assessment, 23*(3), 805.

Swinkels, S. H., Dietz, C., van Daalen, E., Kerkhof, I. H., van Engeland, H., & Buitelaar, J. K. (2006). Screening for autistic spectrum in children aged 14 to 15 months. I: the development of the Early Screening of Autistic Traits Questionnaire (ESAT). *Journal of autism and developmental disorders, 36*(6), 723-732.

Treating Autism & Autism Treatment Trust (2013, March). *Medical Comorbidities in Autism Spectrum Disorders*. London: Treating Autism Publications. Retrieved month day, year, from http://www. treatingautism.co.uk Uljarevic, M., & Hamilton, A. (2013). Recognition of emotions in autism: a formal meta- analysis. *Journal of autism and developmental disorders, 43*(7), 1517-1526.

Ulrich, D. (2000). *Test of Gross Motor Development – Second Edition (TGMD-2)*. Austin, TX: ProEd, Inc.

Ventola, P. E., Oosting, D. R., Keifer, C. M., & Friedman, H. E. (2015). Toward Optimal Outcome Following Pivotal Response Treatment: A Case Series. *The Yale Journal of Biology and Medicine, 88*(1), 37–44.

Warren, Z., McPheeters, M. L., Sathe, N., Foss-Feig, J. H., Glasser, A., & Veenstra-VanderWeele, J. (2011). A systematic review of early intensive intervention for autism spectrum disorders. *Pediatrics, 127*(5), e1303-e1311.

Wechsler, D. (2009). *Wechsler Individual Achievement Test (3rd ed.)*. San Antonio, Texas: NCS Pearson.

Wechsler, D. (2012). *Wechsler Preschool and Primary Scale of Intelligence – Fourth Edition*. San Antonio, TX: NCS Pearson.

Wechsler, D. (2014). *Wechsler Intelligence Scale for Children – Fifth Edition*. San Antonio, TX: NCS Pearson.

Wetherby, A. M., & Prizant, B. M. (2002). *Communication and symbolic behavior scales: Developmental profile*. Paul H Brookes Publishing.

White, S. W., Keonig, K., & Scahill, L. (2007). Social skills development in children with autism spectrum disorders: A review of the intervention research. *Journal of autism and developmental disorders, 37*(10), 1858-1868.

Wiig, E. H., & Secord, W. (1989). *Test of Language Competence – Expanded Edition*. San Antonio: Psychological Corporation.

Wiig, E. H., Secord, W., & Semel, E. M. (2004). *CELF preschool 2: clinical evaluation of language fundamentals preschool*. Pearson/PsychCorp.

Williams, D.L., Goldstein, G., & Minshew, N.J. (2006). Neuropsychologic functioning in children with autism: Further evidence for disordered complex information processing. *Child Neuropsychology, 12,* 279–298.

Williams, D. L., & Minshew, N. J. (2010). How the brain thinks in autism: Implications for language intervention. *The ASHA Leader, 15*(5), 8-11.

Williams, K. T. (2007). *Expressive Vocabulary Test, Second Edition*. Bloomington, MN: Pearson Assessments.

Williams, J. H. (2008). Self–other relations in social development and autism: multiple roles for mirror neurons and other brain bases. *Autism Research, 1*(2), 73-90.

Wilson, B., Pollock, N., Kaplan, B., & Law, M. (2000). *Clinical Observation of Motor and Postural Skills: Administration and scoring manual, Second edition*. Framingham, MA: Therapro, Inc.

Wingate, M., Kirby, R. S., Pettygrove, S., Cunniff, C., Schulz, E., Ghosh, T., ... & Yeargin-Allsopp, M. (2014). Prevalence of autism spectrum disorder among children aged 8 years-autism and developmental disabilities monitoring network, 11 sites, United States, 2010. *MMWR Surveillance Summaries, 63*(2).

Woodcock, R. W., McGrew, K.S., & Mather, N. (2001, 2007a). *Woodcock Johnson III Tests of Cognitive Abilities.* Rolling Meadows, IL: Riverside.

Woodcock, R. W., McGrew, K.S., & Mather, N. (2001, 2007b). *Woodcock Johnson III Tests of Achievement.* Rolling Meadows, IL: Riverside.

World Health Organization. (2004). *International statistical classification of diseases and health related problems (The) ICD-10.*

Xu, Guifeng. (2013). Maternal diabetes and the risk of autism spectrum spectrum disorders in the offspring: A systematic review and meta-analysis. *Journal of Autism and Developmental Disorders, 44* (4), 766-775.

Zafeiriou, D. I., Ververi, A., & Vargiami, E. (2007). Childhood autism and associated comorbidities. *Brain and Development, 29*(5), 257-272.

Zimmerman, I. Steiner, V., & Pond, R. (2002). *Preschool Language Scale, Fourth Edition (PLS-4).* San Antonio, TX: Psychological Corporation.